THREE HUNDRED YEARS
OF FRENCH ARCHITECTURE
1494-1794

British Library Cataloguing-in-Publication Data
A catalogue record for this book is available from the
British Library

Architecture

Architecture (from the Latin *architectura*, after the Greek *arkhitekton*, meaning chief builder) is both the process and the product of planning, designing, and constructing buildings and other physical structures. It is an incredibly important part of human existence – starting from the simplest aspects of survival, yet also functioning as a cultural symbol, a works of art, and as a means of identification of past civilisations.

Building first evolved out of the dynamics between needs (shelter, security, worship, etc.) and means (available building materials and attendant skills). As human cultures developed and knowledge began to be formalized through oral traditions and practices, building became a craft, and 'architecture' was the formalised version of this craft. In many ancient civilizations, such as those of Egypt and Mesopotamia, architecture and urbanism reflected the constant engagement with the divine and the supernatural. Many ancient cultures resorted to monumentality in architecture (think of the Pyramids at Giza, or the Parthenon at Athens) to represent symbolically the political power of the ruler, the ruling elite, or the state itself.

The architecture and urbanism of the Classical civilizations such as the Greeks and the Romans generally evolved from civic ideals rather than religious or empirical ones – and new building types emerged. Architectural 'style' developed in the form of the Classical orders. The earliest surviving written work on the subject of architecture is *De Architectura*, by the Roman architect Vitruvius in the early first-century CE. According to Vitruvius, a good building should satisfy the three principles of *firmitas, utilitas,* and *venustas,* translating as 'durability', 'utility' and 'beauty'.

Early Asian writings on architecture include the *Kao Gong Ji* of China from the seventh century BCE; the *Shilpa Shastras* of ancient India and the *Manjusri Vasthu Vidya Sastra* of Sri Lanka. The architecture of different parts of Asia developed along different lines from that of Europe; Buddhist, Hindu and Sikh architecture each having different characteristics. Islamic architecture began in the seventh century CE, incorporating architectural forms from the ancient Middle East and Byzantium, but also developing features to suit the religious and social needs of the society. In Europe during the Medieval period, guilds were formed by craftsmen to organize their trades and written contracts have survived, particularly in relation to ecclesiastical buildings. From about 900 CE onwards, the movements of both clerics and tradesmen carried architectural knowledge across Europe, resulting in the pan-European styles Romanesque and Gothic.

In Renaissance Europe, from about 1400 onwards, there was a revival of Classical learning accompanied by the development of Renaissance Humanism, which placed greater emphasis on the role of the individual in society. Buildings were ascribed to specific architects – Brunelleschi, Alberti, Michelangelo, Palladio – and the cult of the individual had begun. Leone Battista Alberti, who elaborates on the ideas of Vitruvius in his treatise, *De Re Aedificatoria,* saw beauty primarily as a matter of proportion, although ornament also played a part. For Alberti, the rules of proportion were those that governed the idealised human figure; 'the Golden mean'.

The notion of 'style' in the arts was not developed until the sixteenth century, with the writing of Vasari. By the eighteenth century, his *Lives of the Most Excellent Painters, Sculptors, and Architects* had been translated into Italian, French, Spanish and English. With the emerging knowledge in scientific fields and the rise of new materials and technology, architecture and engineering further began to separate, and the architect began to concentrate on aesthetics and the humanist aspects, often at the expense of technical aspects of building design. Around this time, there was also the rise of the 'gentleman architect' who usually concentrated on visual qualities derived from historical prototypes, typified by the many country houses of Great Britain that were created in the Neo Gothic or Scottish Baronial styles.

The nineteenth-century English art critic, John Ruskin, in his *Seven Lamps of Architecture* (published 1849), had a representative view of what constituted architecture. Architecture was the 'art which so disposes and adorns the edifices raised by men ... that the sight of them contributes to his mental health, power, and pleasure.' For Ruskin, the aesthetic was of overriding significance. His work goes on to state that a building is not truly a work of architecture unless it is in some way 'adorned'. Around the beginning of the twentieth century, a general dissatisfaction with the emphasis on revivalist architecture and elaborate decoration gave rise to many new lines of thought that served as precursors to Modern Architecture.

Notable among these schools is the *Deutscher Werkbund*, formed in 1907 to produce better quality machine made objects. Following this lead, the *Bauhaus school*, founded in Weimar in 1919, redefined the architectural bounds; viewing the creation of a building as the ultimate synthesis – the apex of art, craft, and technology. When Modern architecture was first practiced, it was an avant-garde movement with moral, philosophical, and aesthetic underpinnings. Immediately after World War I, pioneering modernist architects sought to develop a completely new style appropriate for a new post-war social and economic order, focused on meeting the needs of the middle and working classes.

On the difference between the ideals of architecture and mere construction, the renowned twentieth-century architect Le Corbusier wrote:

> You employ stone, wood, and concrete, and with these materials you build houses and palaces: that is construction. Ingenuity is at work. But suddenly you touch my heart, you do me good. I am happy and I say: This is beautiful. That is Architecture.

Architecture itself has an incredibly long and fascinating history. As long as humans have been around, we have needed places to live, and have sought ways to make these spaces beautiful and functional. As our societies continue to change, so does the architecture which reflects them. It is hoped that the current reader enjoys this book on the subject.

THREE HUNDRED YEARS OF
FRENCH ARCHITECTURE
1494 - 1794

BY

SIR REGINALD BLOMFIELD
R.A., M.A., Litt.D., F.S.A., Etc.

PREFACE

In this short introduction to a great subject I have addressed myself not to architects but to the general reader, and I have endeavoured to indicate the main lines of development of a movement in architecture of great and perennial interest. France is so rich in examples of the period illustrated that it is easy to miss the wood for the trees, and in order to understand French Neo-classic architecture it is essential to place it in relation to the history of the time and to regard it as a consecutive development from its tentative beginnings at the end of the fifteenth century till its dissolution at the end of the eighteenth. The short lists suggest some typical examples with approximate dates, but are in no sense whatever to be regarded as exhaustive. For detailed information I must refer students to my *History of French Architecture*, 1494-1661 (2 vols.) and *History of French Architecture*, 1661-1774 (2 vols.), published by Bell & Sons.

July 1936

CONTENTS

[vii]

CONTENTS

LIST OF ILLUSTRATIONS

LIST OF ILLUSTRATIONS

CHAMBORD. THE STAIRCASE

LA ROCHEFOUCAULD

CHAPTER I

The Italian Expedition, 1494. The first Italians in France. The Justes of Tours. Il Rosso. Primaticcio. The Master-builders. The first quarter of the sixteenth century, a Period of Experiment. Withdrawal of the Italians. Examples.

In the study of Architecture it has to be borne in mind that permanent developments, as apart from fashions of the day, are the result of deep-seated causes that may lie far back in history, and are governed in the long run by national instincts and temperament. If one can only carry one's researches deep enough, it will be found that through all the successive phases of any national architecture, there is a continuous trend in one direction, however much the ultimate result may differ from its first beginnings. The idea that it is possible to break entirely with the past, turn one's back on it and begin again, as if it had never existed, is historically unsound, and movements which are based on this fallacy are foredoomed to failure. That this is so, is shown more clearly in architecture than in any of the arts, because of all the arts architecture is most closely associated with the intimate life of the people that produces it. The cosmopolitan ideal is mischievous and futile, and so long as nations preserve their individuality, so long will that individuality be stamped on the best of their architecture. For instance, there have always been definite and unmistakable differences between the architecture of France and of England, of Italy, Spain and Germany. In the sixteenth century a deliberate attempt was made to italianize French architecture. Yet the final result in the latter part of the eighteenth century was essentially French not Italian, a rather austere version of Neo-classic, when Italy had long been revelling in the orgies of the Baroque.

In the three hundred years of French architecture with which I am dealing in this short summary, the dominating factors were not only " the new fashion," as it was called in England, brought from Italy, but the national instincts left by medieval architecture, and the temperament of the French people themselves. The French have always been fine craftsmen, with an irresistible feeling for form. They possess an alert and lively intelligence, quick to pick up fresh motives, and the capacity to work those motives out in their own way, so that though they may have been of alien origin, in due course these motives become characteristically French. The admirable Gothic architecture of France that sprang into brilliant life at the end of the twelfth century, and superseded the last survival of Roman architecture, was probably due to the influence of the Crusades, to what the French knights had seen in the East ; but the French were not the only Crusaders. Other nations had joined in the Crusades, yet their versions of Gothic were very different. The Gothic of Germany, of Spain, of Italy is as different from that of France as a Frenchman is from a German, an Italian or a Spaniard. The history of the rise and development of Renaissance architecture in France illustrates the same inevitable tendency. New motives of design were introduced into France at the end of the fifteenth century. The French took these motives, worked on them in their own way and, after one hundred years of experiment, developed them into a true vernacular architecture of their own. It was once the fashion to deride the Renaissance and, indeed, Neo-classic architecture in general as an exotic. In a sense it was so, but that was not the whole story. The causes that govern the development of architecture lie deeper than this in countries with a long tradition of civilization, and when such a country has absorbed and

[3]

assimilated a fresh motive, that in its turn becomes its national method of expression.

One more word of caution is necessary in regard to Renaissance architecture. It used to be treated as an isolated movement of the fifteenth and sixteenth centuries, out of relation both to what went before and what followed after. Enthusiastic writers, such as Palustre, have dealt with the architecture of François I as if that and that alone constituted the Renaissance in France, but that architecture was, in fact, only the first experimental stage in a movement which did not reach its complete development till more than two hundred years later.

Medievalism as a living force died with Louis XI. His policy was reversed by his successor, and the end of the fifteenth century saw the first of those wild adventures in Italy, which brought France out of her seclusion into the arena of European politics. The Italian expeditions were politically a failure, yet their indirect effect on France was far-reaching and permanent, because they introduced to the court and aristocracy of France an art and a culture, the existence of which they had hardly realized before the disastrous enterprise of Charles VIII. Here and there Italian artists had

TOMB OF THE CHILDREN OF CHARLES VIII, TOURS

BLOIS. THE STAIRCASE (FRANÇOIS I)

appeared in France before the end of the fifteenth century, and the earliest complete example of Italian art in France is the fine monument of Charles, count of Maine, in the cathedral of Le Mans, supposed to have been executed by Laurana about the year 1475, but the real starting point of the new movement was the Italian expedition of 1494. Charles VIII entered Rome on New Year's Eve of that year, but two years later the French army was driven out of Italy.

Charles died in 1498, but he had done his best to import Italian art into France. Tapestries, books, pictures and statuary were sent from Naples to Lyons and thence to Amboise, and among the artists brought back from Italy were Fra Giocondo, the architect and commentator on Vitruvius, Dominique de Cortonne and Guido Paganino. Dominique de Cortonne (il Boccador) was a maker of models for buildings and in 1530 was paid 900 livres for making models of Chambord, and the castles of Ardres and Tournai, and it seems that these were not designed by him but were made to the instructions of higher authority. A certain Luca Becjeane, described as a " deviseur des Bastimens," appears to have had no opportunity of exercising his skill on anything but aviaries and birdcages, and to a certain extent the first importation of Italian art was a false start. The work of the first batch of Italian artists who came to France was, in fact, limited to ornament. There is little trace of any serious attempt to introduce Italian architecture as apart from ornament into France, and even the " amateur du premier rang," François I, never got far beyond ornament in spite of his passion for building. The Justes, a family of Florentine sculptors settled at Tours, confined themselves to monuments and tombs such as the beautiful monument to the children of Charles VIII in the cathedral at Tours, and the monument to William James, canon of Dol (1502). Louis XII, " father of his people," was not greatly interested in the arts, but François I who succeeded him in 1515 was an enthusiastic amateur, and on his accession there was an irruption of Italian artists into France, some of them good, some of them the failures of Italy, but with the solitary exception of Serlio none of them architects. Il Rosso, the red-haired artist, whom Vasari admired so much, carried out some remarkable decorations in the gallery of François I at Fontainebleau in stucco and painting, and Primaticcio who succeeded him was a considerable artist though not very much is now known of him, and he undoubtedly destroyed some of il Rosso's work at Fontainebleau to make room for his own. Francesco Primaticcio had been sent to François I by Federigo, duke of Mantua, in 1531. Vasari says that in 1540 François sent him to Rome to collect antiques and that Primaticcio brought back with him to France 125 pieces. It seems that il Rosso and Primaticcio were the only Italian artists of something like first-rate ability that the French kings were able to secure. The best known of the Italian craftsmen was a de la Robbia, " Maistre Hierosme de la Robie, esmailleur et sculpteur Florentin," who came to France in 1527. In 1535 he was paid a salary of 240 livres a year, and appears in the Royal building accounts for 1537 as receiving 250 livres for a great roundel of terracotta and enamel over the entrance gateway of Fontainebleau—the roundel was adorned with a grand " Chappeau de Triomphe " surrounded by leaves, flowers and fruits of all kinds, melons, pineapples, pomegranates, grapes, poppies, artichokes, lemons, oranges, peaches, frogs, lizards, snails, and " plusieurs autres," so runs the entry in the comptes for a roundel similar to those at Hampton Court, but larger and enamelled in colours, blue, white, yellow, and green

[7]

in the de la Robbia manner. In 1528-1530 Jerome de la Robbia was at work on the Château de Madrid in the Bois de Boulogne at Paris, one of the most famous buildings of the time, destroyed in 1795, and it appears that he was one of the contractors for the masonry. In 1550 de l'Orme added an upper storey and removed some if not all the terracotta ornaments as unsuitable with masonry. De la Robbia was so disgusted that he left Paris in 1553 and did not return till 1560, when Primaticcio had superseded de l'Orme. He is last heard of in 1565 and died two years later.

The one Italian architect who came to France in the time of François I was Sebastian Serlio, but he seems to have been singularly unsuccessful. He may have designed the Château of Ancy-le-Franc, and that " aile de la belle cheminée " which is the best piece of architecture at Fontainebleau, but Serlio was not happy in France. In the dedication of his " Extraordinario Libro " of architecture to Henri II, published at Lyons in 1551, he says that he found himself in the company of " beasts rather than men at Fontainebleau."

The fact was that in spite of royal patronage, and the costly efforts made by François I himself and his courtiers to introduce Italian architecture, the Italians

FONTAINEBLEAU. THE PAVILION

VILLANDRY

were up against an invincible obstacle in the tradition of the French master-builders, and the fixed determination of the latter not to let any foreigner into their monopoly of building, for the guilds were incredibly arbitrary and exclusive. The enthusiasm for this new manner imported from Italy was confined to the King and the amateurs of the Court, and the outlook of the French people was still medieval. For the first quarter of the sixteenth century the master-builders, the le Bretons, the Chambiges, Pierre Nepveu "dit Trinqueau," the Grappins, the Bacheliers of Toulouse, steeped in their inherited traditions and hostile to any other, were in complete control of all building operations. Proud of their skill in masonry, they were taking liberties with building with disastrous results, such as the failure at Beauvais, where the great tower and the flèche that Jean Vast had reared 500 feet above the crossing of the cathedral, collapsed on Ascension Day 1573, within twenty years of its having been built. The church of Niort built in 1535 simply fell down in 1910. With all their amazing skill in stone-cutting the master-builders possessed little scientific knowledge of construction, and they had, in fact, reached their limit when the new manner was thrust upon them by the

Court in the early part of the sixteenth century. Faced with an alien manner which they did not understand and in their hearts thoroughly disliked, there was nobody to guide them but lordly amateurs, such, for example, as the Cardinal Georges d'Amboise, the builder of Gaillon, and, a little later on, the Court financiers, such as Thomas Bohier who built Chenonceaux (1513-24), Gilles Berthelot who built Azay-le-Rideau, or de Semblançay, who, though 82 years old, was hung at Montfaucon in 1527. These men were enamoured of the highly ornamented buildings they had seen or heard of in Italy, such as the Certosa of Pavia, and, as is the way of enthusiastic amateurs, mistook them for architecture. The result was that the French master-builders went on building great houses according to their own tradition, and the Italian ornamentalists covered the buildings with ornament in the manner of their country, the only manner that they understood.

The state of affairs in the building trades after the Italian expedition and, indeed, till the coming of the architects in the middle of the sixteenth century, was chaotic. The French builders knew their trade as masons, and were capable of working on the traditional lines handed on from father to son. Into the midst of these excellent men, there were suddenly thrust in the early years of the sixteenth century Italian ornamentalists, who understood French architecture just as little as the French builders understood Italian, and the result was only Italian ornament applied to medieval buildings, which, so far as architecture was concerned, could perfectly well have done without it. Moreover whatever the " nouveaux riches " and obsequious courtiers might do, some at any rate of the owners of great ancestral houses were not so enamoured of the new fashions as to be ready to pull down their houses, and rebuild in what was supposed to be the Italian manner. When the château of la Rochefoucauld was being rebuilt, 1522-35, the thirteenth-century keep and the round towers at the angles were left undisturbed, and at Châteaubriand Jean de Laval preserved the donjon when he built himself a new house early in the sixteenth century. Noble owners had no objections to Italian ornament so long as it was a surface affair and did not quarrel with their engrained conservatism, but so far as building was concerned, they stood by the old ways.

Italian artists of reputation were brought to France, but, except il Rosso and Primaticcio, they did little or nothing in France. Cellini left the country in a rage,

Leonardo was too old, Andrea del Sarto, having obtained leave of absence in 1519 on condition that he duly returned to Paris, broke his engagement when he found himself in Florence and never came back, Serlio was seldom if ever employed, and the rest of the Italians were the failures of Italy. So the master-builders continued to build in their traditional manner, and the Italian ornamentalists were let loose with their medallions and arabesques, and their stucco decorations, such as the work of il Rosso in the gallery at Fontainebleau. Chambord, that strange fantastic building in the dreary woodland of the Sologne, is a characteristic example. Il Boccador, the Italian " menuisier," supplied the model and Pierre Trinqueau built the château. Yet no building of the time is more completely French, with its vast conical roofs, its angle towers and its centre pavilion with its lofty lantern. The famous double staircase is not Italian, but an ingenious development of the medieval " vis " or newel staircase. Yet Chambord was built fifty years after Alberti had designed the Church of S. Andrea at Mantua, and almost in the year that Peruzzi was building the Palazzo Albergati at Bologna.

France, though ahead of England, was nearly three-

CHAMBORD. THE CHÂTEAU

FONTAINEBLEAU. BASSIN DES CARPES

quarters of a century behind Italy in reaching any real understanding of the new manner of architecture, and if one considers the methods of building at the time, it is rather wonderful that the French builders did as well as they did. All they had to work to was a model, usually prepared by an Italian in the case of the royal houses, and liberally interpreted, and a " devis " or specification drawn up by the King's " varlet de chambre " (private secretary), who in the reign of François I rejoiced in the melodious name of Florimond de Champeverne, and probably knew as little about architecture as his royal master. The building of Fontainebleau was characteristic of the absence of any coherent organization. In 1528 François decided to rebuild and greatly enlarge Fontainebleau. A long " devis " or specification was drawn up by Florimond, but it is a description of the work to be done, not a detail specification. No reference is made to any drawings ; and when a wall was to be carried on corbels, the devis prescribed that it was to be built " ainsi qu'elle le soulloient d'ancienneté." No fixed contract was made for the work, but prices were agreed with the trades, and when the work was completed it was measured and priced " according to the use and custom of

[13]

Paris " by two master tradesmen in the presence of Florimond and two others. Gilles le Breton, "maçon, tailleur de pierres, demeurant à Paris," contracted for walling, brick or stone, at 50 sols (sous) the "toise " or fathom ; payments were dribbled out to le Breton by a Commissioner of building, and the total amount paid him for his work from 1528-34 was 67,042 livres, 7 sols. No architect had yet appeared to check the measurements or inspect the work. It is no wonder that the King was robbed right and left, and it appears from the account of de l'Orme that the builders built so badly that the royal houses sometimes tumbled down, and that they robbed the King without the least compunction. Moreover, François himself was so unstable and egotistical that, having started on a scheme with wild enthusiasm, he seldom if ever carried it through, and lost interest in his buildings before they were up. Large and costly buildings at Blois, Chambord, Fontainebleau, St. Germain, Villers-Cotterets, la Muette and the château de Madrid followed in quick succession, and du Cerceau, writing a few years later, says that some were already ruinous because the King would not take the trouble to keep them up. In spite of the efforts of successive kings—Charles VIII, Louis XII and François I—Italian architecture was still a costly exotic, an affair of the Court, disregarded and disliked by the people. About 1532 a famous shipbuilder, Jacques Ango, built himself a country house at Varange-ville near Dieppe. There is some Italian detail here and there, but the charm of the manoir d'Ango is its tradi-tional French form, and its use of local materials, flints and clunch ; and this delightful building represents the French people of that time far more than the lordly palaces of François I and his courtiers.

The graceful detail, the picturesque grouping, the wealth of their historical associations, their siting on the banks of one of the most beautiful rivers in Europe, have made the châteaux of the Loire famous through-out the world, and have led people to regard them as the full and final expression of the Renaissance in France. This is a dangerous delusion, because at the root of it lies the fatal misconception that ornament is architecture. A critical study of these buildings will show that they are not the last word of a consummate art, but the rather naïve efforts of beginners striving to express themselves in an unfamiliar language. The reign of François I covers that cycle of thirty years in which, as M. Lemonnier says, " tant de choses furent

essayées, abandonnées, combattues, admirées " with no
definite advance in architecture. ". . . tout se juxtapose,
ou se mêle—génie français, génie du moyen âge, génie
Italien, génie de l'antiquité." The results are often
fascinating in the caprice and fantasy of their detail
—those capitals with stag's heads, for example, in the
chapel of St. Saturnin at Fontainebleau, and there is no
denying the perennial charm of this strange chapter of
uncertain aim and experiment, in its romance, and
even innocence so entirely removed from the conscious
and sophisticated effort of much that poses as art at the
present time. Yet out of this confusion of the sixteenth
century, there will rise a definite development in
which " la tradition du moyen âge et même l'esprit du
temps de François I disparaîtra définitivement devant
le pur classicisme,"[1] not very pure classic, it is true, by
the standards of Greece, yet a genuine reconstitution of
architecture in terms of Neo-classic.

A LIST OF SOME TYPICAL BUILDINGS
1494–1547

The dates, where given, are the approximate dates either of
the beginning of new buildings or of additions and alterations
to existing buildings in the new manner. The dates must be

[1] Lemonnier, *Hist. de France*, ed. Lavisse, vol. i, 338.

MANOIR D'ANGO

AZAY-LE-RIDEAU

taken to indicate the period rather than the exact year, and in many cases are conjectural only.

Domestic Architecture.

Amboise (Indre et Loire), 1496.

Gaillon (Eure), 1501 (destroyed).

Maintenon (Eure-et-Loire), 1503.

Chenonceaux (Indre-et-Loire), 1513.

Blois (Loire), 1515.

Azay-le-Rideau (Indre-et-Loire), 1516-1524.

Chambord (Loir-et-Cher), 1519.

Fontainebleau (Seine-et-Marne), 1528 (begun).

Villers-Cotterets (Aisne), 1532.

Chantilly (Oise), 1527.

Château de Madrid (destroyed 1795), 1528.

La Muette (destroyed).

Chateaudun (Eure-et-Loire).

St. Maur-les-Fossés (destroyed).

Hôtel de Semblançay, Tours.

La Rochefoucauld (Charente), 1522-35.

Ecouen (Seine-et-Oise), 1532.

St. Germain-en-Laye (Seine-et-Oise), 1532.

Manoir d'Ango (Seine Inférieure), 1532.

Hôtel Gouin, Tours
Hôtel Pincé, Angers
Hôtel Lallemant, Bourges
Hôtel Cujas, Bourges   about 1530-50.
Hôtel Bourgtheroulde, Rouen
Hôtel d'Ecoville, Caen, 1538
House of Agnes Sorel, Orléans

THE ROYAL BUILDINGS

Villandry (Indre-et-Loire), 1532.
Fontaine-Henri (Calvados), 1537.
Valençay (Indre), 1540.
La Dalbade, Toulouse $\left.\right\}$ about 1540.
Hôtel du Vieux Raisin, Toulouse
Ancy-le-Franc (Yonne), 1537-42.
Bournazel (Aveyron), 1545.
Beaugency (Loiret) Hôtel de Ville, 1520.
Orléans, House of François I, 1536-50.
  Hôtel de Ville, 1530.
  Hôtel de la Vieille Intendance.

Churches.

  St. Pierre, Caen, choir, 1518.
  St. Martin, Pontoise, 1525 (Seine-et-Oise).
  St. Maclou, Pontoise.
  St. Gervais, Gisors, 1525 (Eure).
  St. Eustache, Paris, 1532.
  St. Etienne du Mont, Paris, choir, 1517.
  The organ gallery, Limoges Cathedral, 1533.
  St. Pierre, Coutances (Manche), 1500-50.
  Tillières, 1534 (Eure).
  Organ gallery, Caudebec (Seine Inférieure), 1559.
  St. Rémi, Dieppe, choir, 1522.
  St. Michel, Dijon, 1537.
  Brou, 1513 (Bourgogne).
  Auxerre, S. Pierre.
  St. Vulfran, Abbeville—door, 1550.

THE ROYAL BUILDINGS

Beauvais, transepts, 1510-50.
Rodez, the façade of cathedral, 1530.

Tombs and Monuments.

Tomb of Charles, count of Maine. Le Mans, 1475.
(1) Children of Charles VIII, Tours, 1506.
(2) William James, canon of Dol (Ille-et-Vilaine), 1507.
Monuments of Louis XII, St. Denis, 1516.
Cardinal Georges d'Amboise, Rouen, 1520.
René II, Nancy, 1520.
François II, duke of Brittany, Nantes.
Philibert le Beau, Brou, 1526.
Louis de Brézé, Rouen, 1536.

> All dates approximate only.

Chap. I. Illustrations.

La Rochefoucauld.
Tomb of children of Charles VIII, Tours.
Blois, the staircase (François I).
Chambord, the château.
    do.   the staircase.
Azay-le-Rideau.
Valençay.
Villandry.
Manoir d'Ango.
Fontainebleau, the Pavilion.
    do.   bassin des carpes.

CHAPTER II

1547–1600

Breakdown of the Medieval Tradition. The coming of the Architects. Philibert de l'Orme. His work and what he did for French Architecture. Jean Bullant and the Triad. Pierre Lescot and Jean Goujon. Check in French Architecture in the last quarter of the sixteenth century. Examples.

So far we have not got very far along the road, but in this fifty years of experiment the French craftsmen had learnt the details of Italian ornament. They could carve salamanders, swans transfixed with arrows, porcupines, fleur de lys, ermines and heads of Roman emperors as well as the Italians themselves, and the Italian artists fade away. The great tradition of French medieval sculpture was still alive ; indeed, the French never lost their grasp of it, but the master-builders still clung to their traditional ways, still built mainly by rule of thumb, with results such as the failures at Beauvais and Niort. It was time that some method and more accurate knowledge was introduced into building.

DIJON. ÉGLISE S. MICHEL

TOULOUSE. HÔTEL D'ASSÉZAT

Moreover, the Humanists of the Renaissance had brought about an enthusiasm for classical scholarship so genuine that it had got beyond mere detail, and was beginning to colour the whole of life, and led to a search in the past for a technique that should give expression in architecture to the enthusiasm of the Humanists in letters. Specialists in design began to disengage themselves from the master-builders, and for the first time there appeared in France the architect as we now understand him, the professional designer of buildings, as apart from the contractor who designed his buildings on traditional lines as he went along, or did not design them on paper at all.

By the middle of the sixteenth century a different class of men had appeared in France, men who devoted themselves to the study of architecture, and in some cases had qualified themselves by study of the antiquities of Rome on the spot. These men were essentially artists, not master-builders. They were pioneers in what was to them an intensely fascinating art, an art which they approached with a zeal and ardour of conviction not inferior in its way to that which inspired Ronsard and du Bellay in literature, or Etienne and Amyot in scholarship. Such a man was Philibert de l'Orme, in some ways the most remarkable of that brilliant group of artists who appeared on the stage after the death of François I, and held it with varying fortunes for the next fifty years.

De l'Orme was born at Lyons about the year 1515, and there are still some fragments of his work in that city, including one of those " trompes," an ingenious kind of vaulting over the re-entering angles of buildings, for which de l'Orme took great credit to himself. When about 20 years old he had the good fortune to catch the eye of the Cardinal de Sainte Croix, while drawing and measuring a triumphal arch in Rome. The Cardinal introduced him to the Pope, who gave him some little work, but de l'Orme returned to Lyons in 1536, made the acquaintance of the Cardinal Jean du Bellay, and through him came under the notice of the Court and of the Dauphin (afterwards Henri II), and began a career the success of which was unbroken till the crash of his fortunes that followed the death of Henri II. In due course he became abbé of Ivry and Noyon and a canon of Notre Dame in Paris. His enemies stated that he had been in receipt of 20,000 livres a year when in the King's service, to which de l'Orme indignantly replied that he had been actually out of pocket. He declined to assist the monks at Noyon when they wished to rebuild their abbey. On the other hand, he left a provision in his will for his illegitimate son and daughter.

De l'Orme seems to have gained the favour of Henri II during the lifetime of François I. The King and his son hated each other, and probably for this reason François never employed de l'Orme ; but after the accession of Henri II, de l'Orme won the patronage of Diane de Poitiers, the all-powerful mistress of the King, and as long as the King lived his position was assured. His first work was St. Maur-les-Fossés for the Cardinal Jean du Bellay, on the banks of the Marne near Charenton, a great house with an internal court. De l'Orme was fresh from Italy when he designed the house, and here he introduced the loggias with columns and arcades that he had seen in the palaces of Rome.[1] He designed part of Meudon, and was employed on the various royal palaces, such as Fontainebleau, Villers-Cotterets, and St. Germain-en-Laye. In 1552 he was entrusted with the design of the great house of Anet on the Dure for Diane de Poitiers. Here he introduced many of his

[1] St. Maur-les-Fossés came into the hands of Catherine de Médicis and was sold to her creditors on her death in 1589. It was destroyed before the French Revolution.

ingenious devices, some from the antique, such as a crypto-porticus on the garden side, a circular chapel and other elaborate details which would have been better omitted, but the design of the building, if over-elaborate, was serious, and considered as a whole, it was a genuine attempt at rhythmical and symmetrical composition, different in kind from charming but haphazard buildings, such as Azay-le-Rideau and Chenonceaux.

Henri II succeeded to the throne in 1547 and at once appointed de l'Orme architect at Fontainebleau, the Château de Madrid, Villers-Cotterets, St. Germain-en-Laye, and Yerre, and in 1550 de l'Orme, now a great personage, appears in the accounts as " noble personne, maistre Philibert de l'Orme, abbé d'Ivry, de Saint Barthélemy de Noyon, et de Geveton, conseiller, aumônier ordinaire du Roi, architecte du dit Seigneur, commissaire ordonné et député sur le fait de ses basti-ments et édifices," but in 1559 Henri II was accidentally killed at a court tournament, thrust through the eye by the lance of Montgomery, and with the death of the King de l'Orme's fortunes crashed. The new King François II dismissed him from all his appointments except the tomb of François I at St. Denis. With him

ANET

CHENONCEAUX

were dismissed his brother Jean, " maistre des œuvres de maçonnerie en France," and Jean Bullant, and the entire control of the royal buildings was handed over to Primaticcio, who was not an architect at all. Being now in disgrace, with nothing to do, de l'Orme began his gigantic book on architecture, which, though " fort indigeste et confuse," as he said himself of Vitruvius, was the first really practical modern treatise on architecture. Much of what he wrote was the result of his personal experience and observation, and dealt with problems of construction, stereotomy and the properties of materials. A sense of personal grievance underlies every page of his book, and a temper, always under imperfect control, blazes up in the concluding paragraphs in which he describes, first, the good architect, and then the bad one, the man without hands, blind, stupid and incompetent.

De l'Orme was given one more chance after his fall. Catherine de Médicis employed him on a vast scheme of enlargement of Chenonceaux, begun by Bohier between 1513 and 1524. The only part built of de l'Orme's design was the gallery 180 feet long, which was never completed. His last and most important work was the Tuileries, which, with all its faults in detail, was the largest and most complete palace designed by any one man since the palaces of Imperial Rome. Its general plan was an oblong about 807 feet long by 500 feet wide, with its long axis at right angles to the river. This was divided into three courts, and the general façade was to consist of a ground floor with a loggia and arcade, above which was an elaborate attic storey. The Tuileries was burnt to the ground by the Commune in 1871. It was never a very satisfactory building, as de l'Orme's successors paid little attention to the original design.

De l'Orme died on a Sunday evening in his canon's house at Paris, on January 8, 1570. He had played a great part, written an immense book, and designed some of the most notable buildings in France of the middle part of the sixteenth century. What place does he hold among famous architects ? His own opinion was that he had simply re-established architecture in France. " Have I not also," he says, " done a great service in having brought into France the fashion of good building, done away with barbarous manners and great gaping joints in masonry, shown to all how one should observe the measures of architecture, and made the best workmen of the day, as they admit themselves ? " His enemies asserted that de l'Orme had done very well for himself, but de l'Orme declared that he had saved the

King untold sums and was in fact out of pocket through his efforts. He did actually revolutionize building construction in France, and here he stands apart from his contemporaries, for Lescot, the elegant Court gentleman, left these vulgar matters to his builders and assistants, and Bullant, fine artist as he was, approached architecture too exclusively from the aesthetic standpoint. As a constructor, de l'Orme was far ahead of his time. As an architect he occupies a different position. His art was never spontaneous. It smelt of the lamp, even of the spade and shovel. Through want of imagination he allowed himself to be entangled in details, but though not a great artist, he played a very important part in the development of French architecture and a perennial interest attaches to his strong and unusual personality. It was by his forceful individuality, rather than by his art, that de l'Orme won and has maintained his place among the famous Frenchmen of his time.

Jean Bullant has been described by M. Lemonnier as " un de l'Orme un peu amoindri." So far as I read him, Bullant was nothing of the sort. In their life, their work, and their temperament, Bullant and de l'Orme were quite unlike each other, and the description does less than justice to the most daring thinker in architectural design that France produced in the sixteenth century.

Bullant was born at Ecouen somewhere about 1515, and Ecouen was the house of that great nobleman, and arrogant, obstinate and unpleasant person, Anne, duc de Montmorency, Constable of France, who after a long and eventful life was killed fighting at St. Denis in 1566. But with all his faults Montmorency was a lordly patron of the arts. In his great house at Ecouen he employed Bullant, Jean Goujon, Bernard Palissy, Abaquesne, the potter of Rouen, and the Lepots, the glass painters of Beauvais. Bullant lived among artists and on friendly terms with all, unlike de l'Orme who devoted his attention to the Great Persons of the Court and abused other artists impartially.

At Ecouen Bullant added some very remarkable frontispieces to the existing building between 1540 and 1550. His next work was at Fère-en-Tardenois (Aisne), where the Constable possessed a fine castle of the thirteenth century. Opposite the castle was a plateau admirably adapted for the manœuvres of troops, but it was separated by a steep ravine. Nothing daunted, the Constable called in Bullant to throw a great viaduct, carrying two galleries, 200 feet long, across the ravine

ÉCOUEN

CHANTILLY. THE CHÂTELET

from the castle to the Place d'armes; on the whole, about the best thing Bullant ever did.

In 1557, Bullant was appointed a controller of building operations at a salary of 1200 livres a year, " comme personnage grandement expérimenté en fait d'architecture," and was employed in 1560 by the Constable to build the Châtelet or Petit Château at Chantilly. In 1570 he was appointed to succeed de l'Orme at the Tuileries and at St. Maur. At the Tuileries he built additions to the north and south of de l'Orme's building, with façades of two storeys and an elaborate attic storey. The design was an improvement on that of de l'Orme, but the Tuileries could never have been a satisfactory building. Catherine de Médicis was always in debt and constantly interfered with the design, and the additions made by du Cerceau, le Vau and D'Orbay in the next one hundred years made bad worse, due, as Blondel said, " to the fury with which architects are devoured, of wishing to build something new, when all they have to do is to imitate what is there," a criticism that applies to much modern architecture as well.

In 1572 Catherine de Médicis abandoned the Tuileries, in consequence of the prediction of a fortune-teller that she would perish under the ruins of a house and that St. Germain would be fatal to her. The Tuileries was in the parish of St. Germain l'Auxerrois, and that was enough for Catherine, who stopped the building of the Tuileries, and bought and rebuilt the Hôtel de Soissons in the parish of St. Eustache.

There is only one more important building which may have been designed by Bullant, and that is the Chapelle Funéraire built at Anet after the death of Diane de Poitiers (1566) and completed before 1577. It is a fine simple design, better and more mature than any of de l'Orme's work at Anet, and remarkable for its resolute refusal of all merely technical ornament in the interior. It is not known who was the architect, but Jean Bullant was, I think, the only man of his time who could have designed it. He died in 1578, a month after the death of Lescot.

Of the famous " Triad," de l'Orme, Bullant and Lescot, Bullant was the most original and the finest artist. He started with less advantages than either Lescot or de l'Orme, but his natural genius carried him to a point never reached by either. Lescot, even if he designed his own buildings, as to which I am very sceptical, was uninspired and his work was only saved by Goujon's sculpture, and by a precision of execution which, I am convinced, should also be attributed to Goujon. De l'Orme, a sincere student of architecture but a pedant, mistook knowledge for imagination. He fell into the pitfall which has entrapped many an architect, the snare of archaeology. Bullant was first and last an artist. In all his works it is possible to trace an original idea, a serious attempt to realize some great architectural conception. He was not exempt from the prevailing weakness for the details of antiquity, but whereas to other men detail was everything, Bullant's imagination moved in larger spaces. He was learning the lesson of architecture as the art of great forms and rhythmical proportion. Moreover, he was true to the finest instinct of French genius, the severe restraint which had been the glory of French art in the thirteenth century, and which later on will dignify and ennoble the art of men such as François Mansart and the younger Gabriel. He realized that in architecture some touch of greatness, an aim at heroic scale, the μέγεθός τι of Greek tragedy, is an essential element. It must rise above the multiplicity of details, to unity of effect and a noble simplicity of statement. Just as Goujon raised French sculpture to a plane that it had not occupied since the great day of medieval art, so

Bullant, his friend and fellow-worker, was feeling his way to a conception of architecture as an austere art with its own technique and its own peculiar methods. It is not so much in his actual attainments, as for his brave endeavour and his respect for the dignity of his art, that Jean Bullant ranks with Goujon as one of the bright particular stars of French art in the sixteenth century.

Few men have done so little for their reputations as Pierre Lescot, sieur de Clagny, abbé of Clermont, canon of Notre Dame, the official architect of the Louvre, the friend of Ronsard and of most of the important people of the Court. He was born in Paris about 1510 and came of a legal family of some distinction. Ronsard in a wordy panegyric says that François I loved him more particularly, and that Henri II, a King not conspicuous for scholarship, honoured him so much that he made him his favourite table companion, in fact, that it was a great condescension on the part of a man in Lescot's position to have anything to do with architecture at all. It appears that he had some knowledge of painting, but nothing is known of his training ; there is no evidence that he went to Italy, nor did he produce any works on architecture such as those written by Bullant and de l'Orme.

ROUEN. MONUMENT TO GEORGES D'AMBOISE

ROUEN. MONUMENT TO LOUIS DE BRÉZÉ

PIERRE LESCOT

Lescot first appears on the scene in connection with the rood loft of St. Germain l'Auxerrois between 1540 and 1544. In this work Lescot "discovered" Goujon, and it will be found that in every work in which Lescot was engaged, he associated with himself Jean Goujon. The two collaborated in the famous Fontaine des Innocents in 1550.[1] In 1547 Lescot was appointed architect for the rebuilding of the Louvre, and in 1549 was instructed to prepare a new design and specification. Though Goujon did not appear on the scene officially till 1555, it is probable that he was the "ghost," the architect "sous clef," to use Saint-Simon's phrase in connection with J. H. Mansart, who was mainly responsible for the designs. The architecture is not particularly attractive. It is Goujon's sculpture that gives its real interest and value to the sixteenth century work in the Louvre, the Hall of the Caryatides, the admirable treatment of the vault of the staircase, and the figures and trophies on the upper storey facing the Court. Lescot was in charge up to 1568, but after that date there is no mention of him in the Comptes, and nothing further is known of his work at the Louvre between 1568 and his death ten years later. The last

[1] Taken down in 1785, and rebuilt on an altered plan.

payment made to Goujon was made in 1562 ; after that he disappears from the accounts and from France ; and for long he was supposed to have been killed in the massacre of St. Bartholomew, but he was at Bologna in 1563, and died there before 1568. The year 1562 was disastrous for those of the reformed religion. There were massacres of Huguenots at Sens and Tours, ten years before the Eve of St. Bartholomew. A namesake of Jean Goujon was hanged at Troyes in that year. It was no longer safe for Protestants in France, and it appears that Goujon had to flee for his life and take refuge in Italy. Lescot is not credited with any designs after Goujon had fled and the inference seems to me that Goujon was the designer of the buildings attributed to Lescot, and that the latter was the accomplished and influential amateur at Court who collected the work, saw it through and drew a salary of 1200 livres a year for some two-and-twenty years of his life. I take him to have occupied a position not unlike that of Sir Reginald Bray in England, to whom the design of Henry VII's chapel at Westminster was once assigned without any real evidence.

After the Massacre of St. Bartholomew (1572) nothing seemed to prosper in France. In 1588 Guise and his brother, the Cardinal, were murdered ; Catherine de Médicis died bewildered and uncared for at Blois, and in 1589 the last of the Valois was assassinated by Jacques Clément. It was the end of a dynasty, not only of kings and queens but of artists and scholars. The last quarter of the sixteenth century was almost a blank in architecture in France. The du Cerceau family, Baptiste and Jacques, sons of the famous draughtsman Jacques Androuet du Cerceau, carried on as architects. Baptiste designed the great house at Charleval in Normandy and the Pont Neuf at Paris. His brother Jacques and a cousin, a de Brosse, designed Verneuil near Senlis, begun in 1570, and now in ruins, and they all seem to have been engaged on the Louvre. The last twenty years of the sixteenth century were a desolate waste, and la Bruyère's criticism of Ronsard that he had done more harm than good, because he had severed his art from the people, applied also to the French architects. The fact was that the architects who had superseded the master builders had lost touch with the people and gone too far ahead. They had undoubtedly improved the planning of buildings, first by the quadrangular court instead of the irregular enclosure and more or less haphazard buildings of the medieval

[35]

château built for defence, and from this they had advanced to the open court, with one side open as at Ecouen and the symmetrical façade as at the Château de Madrid (shown in du Cerceau's engraving). They had vastly improved the technique of their art, but they were overburdened with their own knowledge and too anxious to display their mastery of classical detail as then understood. They had not got beyond the stage of considering the orders, that is the Doric, Ionic, and Corinthian orders of columns, as the last word in architecture, and their art was not yet the expression of practical purposes in terms that appealed to all. De l'Orme and his contemporaries had broken up the old tradition, but they had not yet built up a new one in its place. The next step was to make of Neo-classic a true vernacular art, the complete and individual expression of the French genius, and this was to be done under Henri IV, the best King that ever sat on the throne of France.

THE END OF A DYNASTY

A LIST OF TYPICAL BUILDINGS (1547–1600)

Ecouen (Seine-et-Oise), 1547.
St. Germain-en-Laye, 1539-48.
Fontainebleau.
Meudon (destroyed).
The Louvre, from 1550.
Chenonceaux, the gallery, 1556-1576.
Anet, 1552 and 1577.
The Tuileries, begun 1564, destroyed 1871.
Fère-en-Tardenois (Aisne), 1553.
Chantilly, the Châtelet, 1560.
Compiègne, the Porte Chapelle.
Charleval, 1568 } destroyed.
Verneuil, 1575 }
Hôtel d'Assézat, Toulouse, 1557.
Hôtel Bernuy, Toulouse.
Hôtel du Vieux Raisin, Toulouse.
La Rochelle, Maison Henri II.
La Rochelle, Hôtel de Ville.
Nancy, Porte de la Citadelle, 1598.
La Grosse Horloge, Rouen.

Churches.

St. Etienne du Mont, Paris.   The Jubé.
St. Michel, Dijon.
Montargis (Loiret), the choir, 1550.
St. Maclou, Pontoise.
The Chapel of the Valois, Paris (destroyed).
St. Germain l'Auxerrois.

THE END OF A DYNASTY

Tombs.

    St. Denis, Paris.
        François I.
        Henri II.
        Urn—François I.
    Fontaine des Innocents, Paris, 1550 and 1860.
            All dates approximate only.

Chapter II. Illustrations.

    Chenonceaux.
    Anet.
    Ecouen.
    Chantilly, the Châtelet.
    Rouen, monument to Cardinal Georges d'Amboise.
        do.   monument to Louis de Brézé.
    Dijon, Eglise St. Michel.
    Toulouse, Hôtel d'Assézat.

CHAPTER III

1600–1661

Henri IV. Encourages Architecture and the Arts. Town Planning Schemes. Paris. The ' Porte et Place de France'. De Brosse and the Luxembourg. Lemercier and Richelieu, the Town and Château. Le Muet and Tanlay. François Mansart. Balleroy. Blois. Maisons. The Val-de-Grâce. Jesuit Architecture. Examples.

The civil wars had reduced France to a condition of complete exhaustion. " France and I," Henri IV wrote in 1598, " have need of a breathing space." The kingdom was in debt to the extent of 160 millions of francs. It took all the genius and resolution of Henri and his minister Sully to restore order and re-establish the finances of France on anything like a working basis, and they had hardly completed their labours when the King was assassinated by Ravaillac. Considering the state of the country, what Henri IV actually achieved in the last ten years of his life is amazing, and there is a marked distinction between Henri IV and his predecessors. The Valois kings had built to amuse themselves, with complete disregard of the exigencies of the State, and their selfishness was incredible. Henri IV was first and last a patriotic Frenchman, and he pursued a definite policy of encouraging architecture and the arts for the good of the State. In the reign of François I and Henri II a few Italian artists had been lodged in the Hôtel de Petit Nesle across the river, on the site of what is now the Institut de France, but the establishment was broken up in 1559. In completing the Grand Gallery of the Louvre, the express object of Henri IV was to find lodging for artists of all sorts, all Frenchmen if possible, and so establish " une pépinière d'œuvriers," as he called it, a nursery of the arts for the service of the State. He sent artists to Rome, and this was the germ from which sprang the French Academy at Rome, established by Colbert sixty years later. Almost the first work that Henri undertook was a scheme to reorganize Paris. He found that city in a condition of medieval decrepitude, and in 1600 an ordinance was issued for the enlargement, alignment and paving of streets, and the prohibition of overhanging storeys. In 1608 a far-reaching scheme was begun for the improvement of Paris. The Pont Neuf was completed,

LISIEUX. THE ÉVÊCHÉ

LISIEUX. THE ÉVÊCHÉ

PLACE DES VOSGES

and the Place du Pont Neuf begun ; the Place Royale (now the Place des Vosges) was laid out and built, followed by the Place Dauphine (1607) and a splendid scheme of town-planning was drawn up, known as that of the " Porte et Place de France." This scheme provided for an imposing gateway, the Porte de France, of brick and stone, on the north side of Paris. The traveller passing through this gate found himself in a great semicircular space, 480 feet wide at the base, round which were to be ranged seven blocks of buildings separated by streets to which were given the names of the principal provinces of France. At the back of these blocks were gardens, and at a distance of 240 feet there was to be a concentric road, from which twenty-four streets were to radiate right through Paris. One street, for example, starting from St. Denis, was to come to the Pont Neuf, cross the bridge and so out to the southern boundary of the city. The scheme was one of the finest and most comprehensive pieces of town-planning ever conceived. The work was started in 1609, but after the King's murder it was dropped. Richelieu took it up again in 1626, but had his hands too full to carry it through, and the work was finally abandoned.

Henri deliberately encouraged building in order to

give employment and help in settling the country. He completed the Grand Gallery connecting the Louvre with the Tuileries from the designs either of Louis Metezeau or Etienne du Perac, and Jacques Androuet du Cerceau, second son of the old engraver. The probability is that du Perac designed the earlier part next the Louvre, and that the greater part of the Grand Gallery, the strange design of a series of coupled pilasters with pediments, was the work of du Cerceau. The Cour Henri IV, a rather attractive group of buildings, was built at Fontainebleau, a good example of that excellent and unpretentious manner of building in brick and stone which was introduced in the reign of Henri IV, and remained for the next fifty years the vernacular style in less ambitious country houses. Scarcely less important were the buildings at St. Germain-en-Laye. Here the buildings left by de l'Orme were enclosed by a new façade on the river front, and a prodigious series of terraces and stairs was constructed leading down to the river some 320 feet below.

It was also part of Henri's policy to encourage his court to build. Sully built himself a house at Rosny. Lesdiguières, one of the ablest of Henri's officers, had a great house built for him at Vizille (Isère) 1611-20.

Montgomery Ducey, a few miles south-east of Avranches, is an interesting fragment of a house of this period begun but not completed ; and now for the first time since the fifteenth century the French architects developed a vernacular domestic architecture in brick and stone, that is, a manner of design which was used by everyone as a matter of course and without question. The superabundant ornament that had delighted the noblemen and the successful tax-gatherers of the reign of François I was dropped completely. The incessant use of the orders with their unnecessary pilasters was abandoned, and this was a marked advance on the architecture of the sixteenth century, which had been largely experimental and exotic. French architecture steadily developed along these lines till the middle of the seventeenth century. It is regrettable that this excellent manner, based on practical purpose and the considered use of materials, gradually gave way to the more pompous architecture of Italy, but Marie de Médicis, mother of Louis XIII, was an Italian, and after the death of Henri IV, and partly as the result of their studies in Italy, by the middle of the seventeenth century some of the French architects swung back to the Italian motive, and Neo-classic architecture according to the rules of Vignola definitely established itself in France, for we have now reached the era of the text-book. Serlio, Palladio, Vignola and Scamozzi had produced treatises on architecture which found the key to the mysteries of architecture in the " orders," and in official architecture the French architects did not dare to deviate widely from the rules laid down by these writers.

Salomon de Brosse began the Luxembourg for Marie de Médicis in 1615, a large and rather ponderous palace, but he fell out with the Queen over his claims for payment and was superseded. He designed three other important buildings in Paris : the west front of St. Gervais, begun in 1616, a commonplace design ; the Protestant temple of Charenton, destroyed after the revocation of the Edict of Nantes ; and the hall of the Palais de Justice in 1622. He also designed some large country houses, Coulommiers-en-Brie, Liencour and Monceaux, all of them destroyed, and the same rather clumsy technique appears in all of them, to judge the designs by the engravings of Marot and Silvestre. The best thing that de Brosse did was the Parliament House, now Palais de Justice, at Rennes, with its fine hall, 125 feet by 40 feet wide, covered with a waggon ceiling all

VAL-DE-GRÂCE (INTERIOR)

in wood. De Brosse died in 1626. Technically he was
quite competent, but he was heavy of hand, and it is no
use looking to him for the finer qualities of architecture.

Jean du Cerceau designed the Hôtel de Sully, and
when in 1635 Louis XIII bought the Isle St. Louis, some
of the best houses in Paris, such as the Hôtel de Breton-
villers, were built here between 1635 and 1658. The
du Cerceau family are a typical example of the French
custom of father following son in the practice of architecture. The dynasty began with the famous engraver
and survived at least two generations though without
conspicuous success. Much the ablest architect of the
first half of the seventeenth century, apart from François
Mansart, was Jacques Lemercier, one of the best architects in France in the seventeenth century. Not only
did he design a magnificent château for Cardinal
Richelieu, now almost entirely destroyed, but he
designed for him the delighful little town of Richelieu
to house his suite and attendants, an almost unique
example of a complete town built right away and at one
time from the designs of a single architect. He also
designed the churches of the Oratory and St. Roch in
Paris, and in 1635 Richelieu laid the first stone of the
Sorbonne, the most memorable work by Lemercier that

now remains, and technically the most correct building so far erected in France.

Jacques Lemercier was born at Pontoise in the latter part of the sixteenth century and is said to have spent a considerable time in Rome between 1607 and 1620, when he returned to France. In 1628-9 he was employed by Richelieu to design him the Palais Richelieu, now the Palais Royal, and carried out important additions and modifications in the Louvre for Louis XIII. A little later he designed for the Cardinal the vast château and the little town of Richelieu. He superseded François Mansart at the Val-de-Grâce and in 1653, the year before his death, he designed the church of St. Roch. He died in Paris in 1654. For the last twenty years of his life he had been the leading architect in France. He had been Richelieu's right-hand man, and the official Court architect, hardly a man of genius, but a very skilful architect who thoroughly knew his business and a perfectly honest man.

His contemporary, Pierre le Muet, designed Chavigny in Touraine and Pointz in Champagne, both of which are destroyed, and also the great house of Tanlay in Burgundy, surrounded by its broad moat of clear running water, one of the most attractive country houses in France. He also designed some important Hôtels in Paris, such as the Hôtels Davaux, de Chevreuse, and de l'Aigle ; but he outlived his generation and was passed by the younger men. He died in 1669. Without being a first-rate architect, he appears to have been a very capable man, but history has treated him unkindly and, except for his book on building, he would be little more than a name to a few industrious students.

The one really great architect of the seventeenth century was that strange creature, François Mansart. He was born at Paris in 1598, the son of a carpenter in the royal employment. It is not really known how and where he was trained, or whether he ever went to Italy at all, but as d'Argenville, his biographer, said, this was the less material owing to his rare natural endowments, " his exquisite taste, just and solid intelligence, aiming always at proportion, and his rich and noble imagination." His portrait, engraved by Edelinck, shows a refined, thoughtful, rather ascetic face, with a·very long nose, a totally different type of face from the full arrogant countenance of his reputed great-nephew, Jules Hardouin Mansart, the celebrated architect of Louis XIV.

FRANÇOIS MANSART : BALLEROY

François Mansart's earliest works were, it seems, carried out in Normandy, such as the fine house of Balleroy (1626), near Bayeux, with its steep roofs and its two pavilions set in advance of the main body, a characteristic motive of Mansart's design. Tilloloy (Somme), once an important house, has been attributed, I think wrongly, to Mansart. It was built in 1645 on the site of a castle destroyed by Richelieu in pursuance of his policy of breaking the feudal aristocracy. Tilloloy is said to have been built by a master mason, Blaise Carbon. Unfortunately it was destroyed by the Germans in 1916, and it is now impossible to discover who designed it; and this was also the fate of Berni, a fine great house which anticipated in its main lines the famous house of Maisons Laffitte. Not far from Balleroy are the remains of a house at Brécy which was never completed, but there remains an elaborate entrance to what was apparently intended to be the forecourt of a magnificent building. Mansart was wholly indifferent to cost. The essential thing to him was to get his ideas realized. On one occasion at Maisons he actually pulled down the wing of a house built from his designs, because he disliked the look of it, and he appears to have been rather intransigent, and much too

BALLEROY

BLOIS. NORTH WING

FRANÇOIS MANSART : BALLEROY

independent for Colbert to trust him with the completion of the Louvre. But earlier in his career he seems
to have done pretty well what he liked.

In 1635 Gaston, duc d'Orléans instructed him to
prepare plans for the complete rebuilding of Blois. The
whole of the north-west side was pulled down, and here
Mansart designed the stately block of buildings that
occupies the whole side of the château opposite the
main entrance, with its noble stone staircase, an early
example of those amazing staircases hanging in the air
as it almost seems, which came into use in the seventeenth century, masterpieces of masonry dependent for
their stability on ingenious combinations of straight
and curved arches and their resultant forces.

Blois was followed by Maisons on the banks of the
Seine, begun for René de Longueil, an unscrupulous
person, who is said to have spent 12,000,000 livres on
Maisons, and who agreed to a condition insisted on by
Mansart, that the architect should be free to alter his
work as and when he liked. As left by Mansart with its
forecourt and its gardens, Maisons must have been the
most perfect example of domestic architecture in
France ; but after belonging to Lannes, who was killed
at Essling, Maisons was sold in 1818 to Laffitte, a finan-

cier and a man of no taste, who broke up the park into building plots, and a M. Thomas, who succeeded him completed the destruction of the grounds with the help of an " architecte paysagiste," skilled in designing what the French choose to call the " jardin anglais," who put the final touch to the barbarities of Laffitte. Indeed, the great houses of France have suffered most lamentably from the bad taste of the nineteenth century. Still the house remains and I regard this and Mansart's building at Blois as the finest examples of domestic Neo-classic architecture in France. Mansart built at least ten great houses in Paris, such, for example, as the Hotel d'Argouge, or Carnavalet. In the entrance front of this house he had to embody the two lion panels by Goujon and two figures. Mansart managed this with admirable address, and this is a good example of his tact, and of the fastidious refinement of his design.

The originality of Mansart's genius is shown in his church work even more than in his houses. Where Lemercier's design, for example, was able but timid, Mansart comes in as a master, the man who completely realized his idea with no suggestion of failure and with no apparent effort. His work has the inevitable unity which is reserved for the creation of genius. In 1632 he designed the church of the Visitation of Ste. Marie in the rue St. Antoine (now a Protestant church), a beautiful interior on a circular plan, one of the most original ventures in post-Gothic church architecture ever made in France. He designed the front of the great church of the Minimes near the Place Royale, now destroyed, and his last and greatest work was the design for the church of the Val-de-Grâce, begun for Anne of Austria in 1645, to form the central feature of a vast monastery which was to be rebuilt to his designs, but the result was a tragedy. Mansart was recklessly extravagant, the Queen Mother, Anne of Austria, was timid and parsimonious, and within a year of the laying of the foundation stone Mansart was superseded by Lemercier. He had fallen out of favour. Lemercier himself was a loyal and honest man, but Mansart, refined and sensitive, an artist to his finger tips, was nowhere with the adventurers who crowded the French court after the middle of the seventeenth century. He was given one more chance by Colbert, when plans were being considered for the completion of the Louvre. Mansart submitted several, and when Colbert told him that he must definitely fix on one for submission to the King, Mansart withdrew his designs. He died four years later, in 1666. Unscrupulous rivals had embittered his latter days, but he was the greatest French architect in the seventeenth century and stands apart from others in the complete accomplishment of his art, his sense of scale, his feeling for proportion, and his splendid simplicity of statement.

The death of François Mansart marks the close of a very interesting and attractive period of French architecture. In the sixty odd years from the time of Henri IV to the beginning of the personal rule of Louis XIV French architecture had followed its own development, unimpeded by state control, unspoilt by the fashion of the day. The public-spirited lead given by Henri IV in town-planning was not followed up, because for the next fifty years important people in French society were too much occupied with political intrigues to pay much attention to the arts. The result was that the arts went their own way, and one finds in that period greater originality and independence than was possible in the severely disciplined art of the reign of Louis XIV. Nicholas Poussin was a better artist than le Brun, François Mansart than Jules Hardouin, his nephew. Moreover the architects had steadily advanced in technique since the days of the Triad ; and it is this combination of greater freedom with greater technical

PARIS. MUSÉE CARNAVALET

POITIERS. LYCÉE HENRI IV

ability that gives a peculiar fascination to the art of the first half of the seventeenth century in France.

There is one development in French architecture of the seventeenth century which should be noted, though it is of historical rather than architectural importance, and that is the renewed activity in the building of churches, chapels and large educational establishments which followed the recall of the Jesuits in 1604. The development of church architecture is one of the most remarkable features of French architecture in the middle part of the seventeenth century. The medieval tradition had held on in churches after it had failed elsewhere. The choir of St. Rémi, Dieppe, is a curious example with its sturdy cylindrical columns, Renaissance capitals and Gothic vaulting. St. Eustache in Paris, begun in 1552 and finished a hundred years later, has flying buttresses and tracery in the windows. The architecture of the cathedral of Blois, begun in 1678, is a flamboyant Gothic; and the cathedral of Orléans, of which Henri IV laid the first stone in 1601, followed a bastard Gothic design from that date till its completion under Gabriel in the reign of Louis XV. There was a strong religious revival in the middle of the seventeenth century. The Queen Mother began the

great church and establishment of the Val-de-Grâce.
The Jesuits were very active and there was a strong
swing-back to Rome. No trained French architect
could get St. Peter's and the Church of the Jesù out of
his head, and so there came the types of church of the
Val-de-Grâce on the one hand, and the Jesuit church
on the other. On their recall in 1604 the Jesuits at once
started their resolute propaganda both in doctrine and
in building, and much as one may dislike their methods,
they undoubtedly did a very remarkable work in educa-
tion. Their best known architect was Etienne Martel-
lange (1569-1641), who was responsible for part, at any
rate, of the designs for the colleges of Le Puy, Moulins,
Vienne, Carpentras, Vesoul, Dijon, La Flèche, Roanne,
Orléans and Lyons. Though not by him, there are still
fine examples of these great establishments, the Lycée
Malherbe at Caen, the Lycée Henri IV at Poitiers, and
the Lycée Corneille at Rouen, all simple workmanlike
buildings, notable chiefly for their dining halls, with
their half-elliptical vaults. The type of the Jesuit
church is familiar, the nave with shallow recesses
between the abutments of the transverse arches with
galleries above ; and on the outside, as a French writer
has described it, " columns in the ground storey between

the three doors, entablature and cornice, columns in the upper storey on either side of the central œil-de-bœuf, triangular pediment at the top, the implacable façade rises identical in every sky." There is an example at Nevers, St. Pierre, and the best examples are the church of Notre Dame de la Gloriette at Caen and the Montmorency chapel at Moulins, with Regnauldin's stately monument in memory of that hapless young nobleman the duc de Montmorency who was executed by Richelieu in 1632.

It has been a fashion to sneer at Jesuit architecture, but in its early days and before the Jesuits had lost themselves in intrigues and worldly ambition, they had evolved a style which was the genuine expression of a far-reaching educational ideal. Theirs was the last serious and sustained effort in France in building churches and colleges.

A LIST OF TYPICAL BUILDINGS
1600–1661

Place des Vosges, Paris, 1604.
Place Dauphine, Paris, 1607.
Gallery of the Louvre and Pavillon de Flore.
Fontainebleau (Cour Henri IV, Chapel).

TYPICAL BUILDINGS

St. Germain-en-Laye.

The Luxembourg, 1615-27.

Vizille (Isère), 1612-20.

Montgomery Ducey (Manche).

Palais de Justice, Rennes, 1624-54.

Palais Royal, Paris, begun 1629-34.

Richelieu (Indre-et-Loire).   The church and town.

Blois, Aile de Gaston d'Orléans, 1635.

Tanlay (Yonne), 1642-47.

Maisons (Seine-et-Oise), 1642.

Balleroy (Calvados).

Brécy (Calvados).

Hôtel Carnavalet, Paris, 1550 and 1660.

The Palais Royal, Paris, 1629-34.

Cheverney (Loir-et-Cher), 1634.

Miromesnil (Seine Inférieure), about 1650.

Thugny (Ardennes).

Beaumesnil (Eure), 1633-44.

Chambray (Eure).

Champ de Bataille (Eure).

Hôtel de Ville, Troyes, 1625.

Pont Neuf, Toulouse.

Rennes, Palais de Justice, 1618-54.

The Lycée, Eu (Seine Inférieure).

Lycée Corneille, Rouen.

Lycée Henri IV, Poitiers.

Eu, le Château.

Lycée Malherbe, Caen.

Auray, Eglise St. Gildas, 1636.

CAEN. NOTRE DAME DE LA GLORIETTE

VAUX-LE-VICOMTE. THE GARDENS

St. Omer, the Jesuit College (now l'Hôpital Militaire).
Cany Barville (Seine Inférieure), 1640-46.
Daubeuf (Seine Inférieure), 1629.
Vaux le Vicomte (Seine-et-Marne), 1653-59.
Bevilliers Breteuil (Seine-et-Oise).
Rosny (Seine-et-Oise).
Suzanne (Somme).
Tilloloy (Somme), 1645.
Hôtel de Vogüé, Dijon, 1614.
Evêché, Lisieux.
Courances (Seine-et-Oise).
Vannes, Hôtel de Limur.

Churches.

St. Omer, Chapel of Lycée, 1615-29.
The Sorbonne, 1635.
Eglise de la Visitation de Ste. Marie, Paris, 1632.
Val-de-Grâce, Paris, 1645.
Nevers, St. Pierre.
Moulins, the Montmorency Chapel.
St. Roch, 1653.
St. Paul, St. Louis, 1627-41.
Notre Dame des Ardilliers, Saumur, 1534-1654.
St. Gervais, Paris, 1616.
Orléans, the Cathedral, 1601-1790.

All dates approximate only.

CHAPTER IV

1661–1708

Colbert's reorganization of the Arts. Le Vau and the transition.
Collége des Quatre Nations. Vaux-le-Vicomte. The completion
of the Louvre. Bernini. Claude Perrault. François Blondel.
The ' Architectes du Roi.' Bruand. Bullet. André le Nôtre.

The third lap in French Neo-classic architecture closes with the death of François Mansart, and we now enter on the prodigious building enterprise of Louis XIV. In the first fifty years of the sixteenth century the master-builders and the Italians were fighting for mastery, and, in the last fifty, the master-builders had to make way for the architects who regularized and, to some extent, standardized the results of the Italian incursions into France. The period from the beginning of the seventeenth century down to the death of Mazarin in 1661 saw the full and mature realization of French Neo-classic architecture. It was not a period of great building activity. The encouragement of architecture begun by Henri IV ended with his death.

Louis XIII was rather lethargic, Richelieu's policy was to pull down a turbulent aristocracy, rather than do anything to increase its powers, and Mazarin was so much occupied with preserving his own position amidst incessant intrigues of the Court, that he paid little attention to architecture, and concentrated his efforts on amassing a vast fortune and a magnificent collection of works of art. Meanwhile however architects had been left free to pursue the development of their art in their own way, and when Mazarin died the technique of French architecture was assured, and everything was ready for the great outburst of building for Louis XIV in the thirty years from 1661 to 1690. The death of Mazarin marks the end of a long and varied chapter in the history of French architecture, and the rise of a new era which differed materially in its methods of organization from that which preceded it.

Mazarin had been content to leave things alone. He interfered as little as possible with the officers of the State, including the architects on the royal staff. François Mansart, le Muet and Lemercier enjoyed much greater liberty of action than Colbert allowed to their successors. Under the official machinery established by Colbert, architects, painters and sculptors

VAUX-LE-VICOMTE. THE CHÂTEAU

LES INVALIDES   *Yvon*

had to do what they were told by the King and his resolute and relentless minister. The King was vain, arbitrary, despotic, and fond of being flattered, with the result that intrigue was rampant at his Court, and however able an architect might be, he was not likely to go very far unless he could secure the favour of the King's minister, or that of one of the royal mistresses. The result was the rather dreary monotony of official architecture. Saint-Simon gives a saying of the time : " Henri IV avec son peuple sur le Pont Neuf. Louis XIII avec les gens de qualité à la Place Royale, et Louis XIV avec les maltotiers [1] dans la Place des Victoires."

When Mazarin died Louis XIV was twenty-two. He was determined to have his own way and govern himself, but he was fortunate in having in Colbert a first-rate minister, who kept him out of mischief with considerable success, largely by diverting his energies into profuse and very costly building. There is no doubt that Louis XIV, like François I, loved building and prided himself on his taste and the accuracy of his eye, but till Colbert took it in hand the condition of the administrative machinery in France seems to have been chaotic.

[1] Tax-gatherers.

In 1653 Fouquet had been appointed " Surintendant des Finances," and his business was not only to receive money but also to raise it. " Il lui (le Roy) prêtait comme particulier, et se remboursait comme surintendant."

Fouquet was an attractive person, but evidently unscrupulous in his methods, and hopelessly extravagant. He is said to have spent 18 million livres on the house and grounds of Vaux-le-Vicomte. It is difficult to fix the value of the livre in the seventeenth century. In 1666 le Brun received an annual salary of 8800 francs, and Bernini 6000 for himself and 1200 for his son, and the salaries of the Architectes du Roi in 1673 varied from 200 to 1200 francs a year. Reckoning the livre at five francs to the pound the cost of Vaux-le-Vicomte would have been between three and four millions sterling. To show his loyalty, Fouquet gave the famous fêtes at Vaux-le-Vicomte in honour of the King, but it was the end of his career. Colbert was determined to destroy him. Fouquet was arrested, and only escaped death through the strenuous exertions of his friends. Colbert made himself Surintendant des Bâtiments in 1664, combining more or less the functions of a First Lord of the Treasury, a Minister of Fine Arts and a First Commissioner of Works. He proceeded to organize a large staff, composed of the leading architects of Paris at the time. Colbert styled himself " Surintendant et Ordonnateur Général des Bâtiments, jardins, tapisseries, et manufactures de France," at a salary first of 15,000 livres a year ; rising under the skilful manipulation of Jules Hardouin Mansart, twenty years later, to 60,886 francs. Under the Surintendant were the various " officiers des Bâtiments," (1) three Intendants, at salaries of 6000 francs a year, (2) three Contrôleurs at 4500 francs a year (André le Nôtre was a contrôleur for the last thirty-two years of his life), (3) three Trésoriers at 2800 francs a year. One of Colbert's instructions begins, " Il faut travailler incessament," and under that iron man his subordinates must have had a difficult time. Below these permanent officials came the architects, paid " pour servir généralement dans toutes les maisons royales," and at the head of the list came Louis le Vau, " premier architecte de Sa Majesté," at an annual salary of 6000 francs. These appointments were eagerly sought for, and could be obtained by purchase or inheritance. They were more or less confined to certain families, their friends and connections, and in spite of Colbert's watchful eye they afforded plenty of opportunities for jobbery. What the elder Gabriel designed, his brother and his uncle contracted for, and some other relation checked the accounts, and the dangerous system of measure and value in use in the sixteenth century seems to have continued under Colbert. Within this ring fence of monopoly, and with direct interference by the Surintendant, there was little room for adventure. François Mansart was the last representative of that old school, free and unfettered, in which men designed according to their own ideas of what was right and not to an iron standard of design. After 1664 no French architect would have dared to treat a royal commission with the casual independence of François Mansart when called in at the Louvre.

From this date forward, French architecture becomes official, to a large extent standardized. The Academy laid down rules for the right use of the orders and other details of architecture. The happy freedom of Fontainebleau, the resolute individualism of the manner of Henri IV, the high ideals of such men as François Mansart, were now to be things of the past. Versailles was the standard, and Jules Hardouin Mansart and le Brun the protagonists of " le bon goust," and we

INSTITUT DE FRANCE

THE LOUVRE. E. FRONT

must look for a period of consummate accomplishment, rarely relieved by flashes of genius.

Scarcely less important than his reorganization of the royal staff was Colbert's establishment of the Academy of Architecture. An Academy of Painting and Sculpture had been founded in 1648, in order to break the monopoly of the guilds of painters and sculptors. Meanwhile, there was no academy of architecture. In 1663 Colbert had established an advisory committee to help him with the Louvre, and in 1664 the first steps were taken to establish an academy in Rome, for students in painting and sculpture, under Poussin. The advisory committee was promoted to the status of a " Conseil des Bâtiments," but this also proved unsatisfactory, and in 1671 Colbert established an Academy of Architecture, to advise him about the royal buildings, to instruct students and to lay down rules for the practice of architecture. The elder Blondel was its first professor, and there can be no doubt that, in its earlier days, this academy did some very useful work, in providing for the training of students, settling technical questions and clarifying the practice of architecture. It gradually established that tradition of thorough training, and sound and scientific building, which was to be the special distinction of French architecture for the next two centuries. Its educational work in connexion with the famous French Academy in Rome was of the highest importance, and it had little difficulty in establishing a severe and uniform gymnastic, because for a hundred years from the date of its foundation there was no serious difference of opinion as to standards and first principles, and as to what is and is not beautiful. It was inevitable that French architecture should become almost entirely academic, in the sense that it had to conform to some definite type. On the other hand, the refinements of the art, proportion, fastidious selection, and skilful planning, were thoroughly mastered. French architecture in the eighteenth century, down to the Revolution, may have been monotonous, but technically it was perhaps the most accomplished that had appeared in Europe since the days of Greece.

The career of Louis le Vau marks the transition from the age of Mazarin to the age of Colbert. Le Vau was born in 1612 and became one of the leading architects in France in the middle of the seventeenth century. About 1656 he rebuilt the south front of the Louvre, and the east front, now concealed behind Perrault's façade, and in 1664 completed and spoilt the Tuileries. He designed the Collége des Quatre Nations (now the Institut de France) shortly before the death of Mazarin, on the whole a fine design considering the difficulties of the site on the south bank of the river, but le Vau's best work was done in the country at Rincy and Turny, two fine great houses, both destroyed, and more particularly at Vaux-le-Vicomte, designed in 1653 for Fouquet, the Surintendant des Finances, with its magnificent gardens by le Nôtre. Vaux-le-Vicomte is still one of the most splendid houses in France. Unlike Maisons, its beautiful setting has been preserved unaltered, and house and grounds give a better idea of a great country-house of the time of Louis XIV than any other in France. In 1661 le Vau was called in to add to the old hunting lodge which Louis XIII had built at Versailles. He added two wings, but the work was stopped in 1664. Le Vau was very unlucky. Nothing more was done at Versailles till some fifteen years later when Mansart swept away all that le Vau had done, and in the same year (1664) le Vau was superseded at the Louvre and passed by younger men, for he belonged to the old régime, to the generation that went out with Mazarin, and though very successful in his day and a fine architect he had never been quite on the level of Lemercier or François Mansart. Le Vau died in 1671. D'Orbay, his son-in-law, was associated with le Vau in his later works, but was not a considerable architect. He was an original member of the Academy of Architecture established by Colbert in 1671, and gave a design for the Porte du Peyrou at Montpellier, carried out by Daviler in 1685. He died in 1697 long passed over and forgotten.

I mentioned before that Colbert in his efforts to keep the King out of mischief, diverted his energies to magnificent building, and began with the completion of the Louvre, at that time in an unfinished and unsatisfactory condition, and it is a remarkable thing that this, the first important architectural undertaking of the new régime, was entrusted not to a professional architect but to a brilliant amateur who had been trained as a doctor. Colbert was very anxious to keep the young King in Paris, and in order to do so, wrote to the King that the time had come " s'appliquer tout de bon à achever le Louvre." Le Vau had been at work at the Louvre since 1656. Colbert now had a model made of his design, and asked the architects of Paris for their opinions on its merits. The architects, instead of standing by their colleague, condemned his design, and produced various designs of their own. Meanwhile, Charles Perrault, Colbert's secretary, produced an anonymous design, made by his brother Claude, and this design was sent to Rome to obtain the opinion of famous Italian architects, Carlo Fontana, Pietro Berrettini, Bernini and others. The Italian architects followed the example of the French, disparaged the design and produced various designs of their own " tous fort bizarres "; but Bernini had the greatest reputation of any architect in the world of his time, and his friends impressed on Colbert that there was only one man living capable of the work, and that was Bernini. Accordingly Bernini was invited to come to Paris by a personal letter from the King himself, and his journey was in the nature of a royal progress. Bernini produced a prodigious design which involved the destruction of the greater part of the existing Louvre, and though it had fine points, it was, in fact, impracticable, but so great was Bernini's reputation that his design was accepted, and the first stone actually laid in October 1665, six months after his arrival in Paris.

Meanwhile, the indefatigable Charles Perrault called Colbert's attention to the numerous faults of Bernini's designs. Indeed on one occasion Bernini caught Perrault spying on his designs, called him a dirty dog, and told him he was not fit to black his boots, and that for twopence-halfpenny he would smash the King's bust and return to Italy. Bernini returned to Italy thoroughly disgusted with France. The fact was that the whole thing was a farce. Colbert probably, and his secretary certainly, never meant to have any but a French architect employed, and Charles Perrault had succeeded in manœuvring his brother Claude into the commission for the completion of the Louvre, and Claude produced one of the most remarkable architectural designs of the seventeenth century. Few buildings have made a greater sensation or aroused more lively controversy than the peristyle of the Louvre, the façade on the east side. The elder Blondel, a rather disagreeable old pedant, condemned Perrault's design with its double columns as having no precedent in antiquity. Hermogenes, he said, might do what he liked with coupled columns or anything else, but Perrault was not a Hermogenes. Blondel might well have criticized Perrault's design for its complete disregard of the existing building and of what poor le Vau had done only a few years before, but Perrault would probably

have quoted Bernini's design as a precedent, for the
Italian had proposed to pull down the whole building.
The younger Blondel, a much better judge, lecturing
fifty years later, pronounced Perrault's design to be
" non seulement le triomphe de l'architecture et de
sculpture, mais encore le chef d'œuvre de l'art, pour la
hardiesse de la construction. Tout y est noble et
imposant." He ranked it with the Porte St. Denis,
Maisons and the Val-de-Grâce as one of the three or
four masterpieces of French architecture, but Perrault's
colleagues were jealous, the King lost interest in the
Louvre, and the work gradually flickered out. The
east and part of the sides only of this great design
were completed. Perrault fell out of favour and died in
1688 of blood poisoning caught in dissecting a camel.
Perrault was a man of brilliant ability, in some ways not
unlike Christopher Wren in his combination of scientific
knowledge with unusual power of invention and a very
original turn of mind. Partly owing to the fact that he
began as an amateur with most inadequate technical
training, Wren did not take up architecture where Inigo
Jones had left it in the reign of Charles I. So Perrault on his part made no attempt to follow in the track
of François Mansart and Lemercier, but went off on a

line of his own, for the peristyle of the Louvre is not quite like any other French work of the seventeenth century.

François Blondel, Perrault's rival, was almost exactly his contemporary, and like Perrault is not known to have received any specific training in architecture, but for three years he was travelling tutor to the son of a secretary of State, and studied the architecture of the various countries which he visited. He was employed for a time by the State as inspector of harbours and certain engineering works, and he seems to have been a good constructor, for the bridge at Saintes, built from his design in 1665, lasted till 1845, when it was taken down ; whereas J. H. Mansart's bridge at Moulins stood up for just five years. Blondel was also a most industrious and conscientious pedant. Like Claude Perrault, he was 52 years of age when he made his first essay in original architecture, but unlike Perrault he was hidebound by what he believed to be antiquity. He could not escape it when he designed the Porte St. Denis, and it coloured the whole of his teaching of architecture at the Academy, and his famous " Cours d'Architecture ". What Blondel prided himself on most of all was his composition of sonorous Latin inscriptions. He was in no sense a great architect, nor was he an attractive writer. He

[72]

endeavoured to establish a rigid and absolute philo-
sophy of art, with fixed laws of architecture, almost as
part of Colbert's State machinery, but his aesthetic was
fantastic and his logic ridiculous. He was untouched
by the literary quality and large tolerance which distinguished the writings of both the Perraults.

In his reorganization of the State machinery Colbert
had established a staff of architects who were in the
King's pay, and were entitled to call themselves
" Architectes du Roi ". Among them were many able
architects who are now almost forgotten, owing to the
astonishing success of Jules Hardouin Mansart, who
succeeded in monopolising all the important work that
was done in France before the end of the prosperous
days of Louis XIV. Charles Errard, Bruand, Pierre
Mignard, Anthoine Lepautre, Cottart, Richer, Robelin,
Gobert, Gittard and le Duc were all architects employed
on one or other of the important buildings erected in or
near Paris in the earlier part of the reign. Liberal Bruand
designed the vast hospital of La Salpêtrière, and in
1675 he was entrusted with the design of the Hôtel de
Mars or des Invalides, that splendid hospital which
Louis XIV had built for disabled soldiers, " les
estropiéz et caducs ". He was undoubtedly an excel-

lent architect, but, like many others of his colleagues, he was elbowed out by Jules Hardouin Mansart, and when he died in 1697 was in serious financial difficulties. Pierre Bullet, who designed the Porte St. Martin, was more fortunate. He continued in active practice almost up to the date of his death in 1716, and the younger Blondel, who knew his work, regarded him as a master in his art. These architect members of the French Academy of Architecture undoubtedly knew their business and had to at their own risk, for there was Colbert waiting grimly in the background, and colleagues anxiously looking out for any blunders that might lead to their supersession. But their position was, to a certain extent, safeguarded by the Academy which tended to become more and more a family affair. The families of J. H. Mansart, Bullet, Bruand, D'Orbay, Gobert, de Cotte and l'Assurance are examples of two generations, and Mollet and Gabriel of three generations of architect members of the Academy of Architecture. Nearly all these " Architectes du Roi " were distinguished men in their time, but with two exceptions we do not find any outstanding figure among them. The two exceptions were men who for good and bad dominated the architecture of the age of Louis XIV, André le Nôtre and Jules Hardouin Mansart.

ILLUSTRATIONS

CHAPTER V

1680–1708

André le Nôtre. The Tuileries. Versailles. Chantilly. Jules Hardouin Mansart. The King's extravagance. Versailles. Maintenon. Marly. The Church of the Dome. Mansart's amazing success.

Two men stand out among the multitude of artists in the reign of Louis XIV, André le Nôtre, the designer of grounds and gardens, and Jules Hardouin Mansart, the architect of Versailles. Le Nôtre was born in 1613, the son of Jean le Nôtre, the official gardener of the Tuileries. He learnt something about drawing in the studio of Simon Vouet, principal painter to Louis XIII with lodging in the Louvre and a large salary. Most of the artists who became famous in the earlier years of the reign of Louis XIV passed through Vouet's studio, and here le Nôtre met le Brun, le Sueur, Mignard and others, and began his career as an artist and designer. The point is important, because it means that le Nôtre had training and knowledge before

[76]

VERSAILLES. THE CHAPEL

THE PETIT TRIANON

he settled down to the design of grounds and gardens, unlike our landscape gardeners and municipal engineers, who assume that they can do these things by the light of nature without any training in design, and even rely on the saying of Lancelot Browne, the famous, or infamous, hero of the " jardin anglais " in the eighteenth century, that " knowledge hampers originality."

In 1637 Jean le Nôtre resigned his post of gardener to the Tuileries in favour of his son André. This was confirmed by a royal brevet, and for the next fifty-five years of his life André was paid an annual salary of 1200 francs a year with a lodging in the Tuileries " pour travailler aux desseins des parterres et jardins de S.M." Charles Mollet, another well-known garden man employed on the royal designs, received only 500 francs. The salary which appears in the accounts year after year till le Nôtre resigned it in favour of his nephew soon became a retaining fee, for in addition to this le Nôtre received an annual salary of 3000 francs as " Contrôleur Général Ancien des Bastiments de S.M.," a post to which he was appointed in 1670-71. In addition to this he received payment for individual work, such as 1500 francs for his care of an " espalier de jasmins d'Espagne " in 1672, and that year he was being paid an

[77]

annual salary of 8000 francs for the care of the gardens and grounds of the Tuileries. One way and another the " officers serving the King," as they were called, managed to pick up very comfortable incomes.

Le Nôtre's work at the Tuileries is specified in detail in the accounts of Louis XIV. His duties were to " clear, beat and rake " the grand terrace in front of the palace and various paths and alleys, to clip and keep in order eight squares " de parterre en broderie " and various beds and borders, to furnish them with flowers in their proper seasons at his own cost, to maintain a flower garden filled with flowers " particularly during the winter," with all necessary heating and mould, and to keep the " espalier de jasmins d'Espagne " in good order. Generally, he was in charge of all the royal gardens, providing designs, arranging for their execution and seeing that they were duly carried out.

In addition to this work, le Nôtre was in constant employment at most of the great houses in the neighbourhood of Paris. In the years 1656-61 he laid out the grounds of Vaux-le-Vicomte, a characteristic example of his manner still much as he left it. Near the house after a low terrace he kept the ground low with " parterres de broderie " on either side of the great central walk leading down to the " canal " running right and left, 3000 feet long and 120 feet wide. Beyond this the ground rises and here le Nôtre designed some prodigious works : an immense grotto with seven great arched recesses ; on either side broad ramps ascended to a plateau on which were to be found elaborate cascades, everything on a scale which must have opened the eyes of the King and Colbert to the extent to which Fouquet had dipped into the moneys of the State. In the beautiful view of the grotto of Vaux by Perelle the design is expressly attributed to Sr. le Nôtre, and this shows that le Nôtre was in fact an accomplished architect, with an extraordinary sense of the possibilities of the sites with which he dealt, an artist on an entirely different footing from that of the modern landscape gardener. In a treatise published in Paris in 1709, *La théorie et pratique du jardinage*, the anonymous author says of gardener designers, " These men conceit that because they can prune a fruit tree and make a kitchen bed, they are perfectly skilled too in what relates to pleasure gardens." This book by the way, a translation of which by James of Greenwich, the architect, appeared in 1712, was a famous book in its time. It is the only complete account of garden design as practised by le Nôtre and his contemporaries, a manner of which the best examples in England are Hampton Court and Wrest.

His design showed a frank disregard of the ways of nature left to its own devices, and the claims for a deification of nature, advanced with such unction by the landscape gardeners of the latter part of the eighteenth century and since, would have had no meaning for le Nôtre and his contemporaries.

His work at Versailles is well known. It is laid out on exact geometrical lines, elaborate parterres in front of the palace, divided into rectangular compartments, a broad central walk leading down to the Bassin d'Apollon and beyond to the great Canal, and from the Bassin d'Apollon straight avenues laid out as a patte-d'oie (goose-foot) lead outwards through bosquets of tall trees to the outer boundaries of the grounds. Fountains, figures, groups of figures, flights of stairs, and all sorts of admirably executed details are found everywhere. The gardens took twenty years to complete and the expense was enormous, for the site was a bad one. In one year, 1680, the cost of earthwork alone was 931,506fr. 9s. 7d., and added to this was the disastrous failure of the aqueduct of Maintenon and the never-ending noise and expense of the machine of Marly, built to throw up water from the Seine into the gardens.

The Grand Condé had retired to Chantilly in partial disgrace, and here he amused himself with laying out an immense garden begun in 1663 from the design of le Nôtre. All that is now left of it is the water garden, and the canal, one of the most interesting gardens in France. The canal is given in an old map as 150 feet wide and 4800 feet long, and le Nôtre adopted the unusual device of substituting waterpieces for parterres. A few years later he designed the gardens, waterpieces and grounds for Colbert at Sceaux (destroyed in 1798), and for Louvois who succeeded Colbert, he levelled and transformed wholesale the high ground surrounding the stately house of Meudon (now destroyed). I imagine at no time in the history of architecture has there been such reckless extravagance in building great houses and having enormous gardens as in those first twenty-five years of the reign of Louis XIV. Sites were selected without the slightest thought of economy and le Nôtre was allowed to do pretty well what he liked, but there is this always to be said for him, that he was intent on his work and never thought of himself.

LE NÔTRE AT ROME

In 1679 he was sent by Colbert to Italy to pick up any new ideas for the Royal palaces. He had introductions to all the best people in Rome, and at an audience with the Pope he rushed forward, kissed the Pope on both cheeks and exclaimed : " Eh, bon jour, mon révérend père, et que vous avez bon visage, et que je suis aise de vous voir en si bonne santé." The Pope was delighted. Le Nôtre was elected a member of the Academy of Architecture in 1681 and attended one meeting. He found the members busy with " the colossal order " and was so bored that he never attended again. He died in 1700 at the age of eighty-seven and one wishes that more was known of him, for he was a simple-minded lovable man without guile of any sort. Saint-Simon says of him : " Le Nôtre avait une probité, une exactitude et une droiture qui le faisaient estimer et aimer de tout le monde. Jamais il ne sortit de son état ni ne se méconnut, et fut toujours parfaitement désintéressé." High praise from that austere critic. Le Nôtre and Vauban, the great engineer, were perhaps the only people at the court of Louis XIV who deserved that praise.

Jules Hardouin Mansart owed his immense and overpowering success to qualities very different from

those which distinguished le Nôtre. He was born in
1645 and his real name was Hardouin, but on his
mother's side he was a grand-nephew of François Mansart, and Saint-Simon says that on the death of that
great architect in 1666 he took the name of Mansart
" pour se faire connaître et se donner du relief," but
Saint-Simon, who hated and despised Mansart for his
familiarity and pretensions, did not do justice to his
energy and unscrupulous thrust, for he was undoubtedly
very able. Jules Hardouin seems to have been a typical
" faux bonhomme," as the French say, the sort of
man who would slap a royal duke on the back, tell
him a coarse story, and in cases get away with it,
for his success was amazing. In 1674, by an obscure
intrigue he managed to supersede Anthoine le Pautre
in the design of Clagny for Madame de Montespan ;
and from that time forward his fortune was made.
He was brought into touch with the King. Colbert
pushed him into the Academy and in 1676 the King
entrusted him with the immense undertaking of Versailles. This meant the end of the old régime and the
definite inauguration of the new. Colbert had failed in
his effort to keep the King in Paris. The works at the
Louvre were abandoned and Louis XIV indulged him-

[83]

self in his hobby of building palaces and country houses at great cost and with complete disregard of the interests of the State.

In the years 1676-90 money was poured out like water on the royal houses and gardens. Mansart, who was extremely astute, had only to flatter the King's vanity and he got what he wanted, for Louis XIV was incredibly vain and believed himself to be an infallible judge of architecture. Saint-Simon says that Mansart used to lay traps for the King and applaud him for his wonderful judgment. It seems that Louis had an accurate eye for detail, but he had no taste, and " ce délié maçon," as Saint-Simon calls Mansart, had him in his hands. Versailles was the first opportunity. The site was naturally a very bad one, " le plus triste et le plus ingrat de tous les lieux," no view, no wood, no water, no earth, for it was all running sand or marsh. Everything had to be brought to the place, and both here and at Marly the King seems to have made a point of showing what he could do with a hopeless site. The cost of Versailles was enormous and never-ending. Against Vauban's advice he insisted on the aqueduct of Maintenon (1685-95) which had to be abandoned after costing nearly nine million francs and

MAINTENON. THE AQUEDUCT

THE ORANGERY AT VERSAILLES

the lives of hundreds of workmen. When Louis began to reconstruct Versailles, there was on the site a hunting-box of Louis XIII, a small and rather charming house of brick and stone in the manner of Henri IV. Mansart transformed this into the gigantic palace of Versailles, of which Saint-Simon says, in my opinion justly, that " la main-d'œuvre est exquise; l'ordonnance nulle ". Much the best thing in the architecture of Versailles is the Orangery, a work in the true grand manner, which in my opinion was probably not Mansart's work at all, but designed possibly from a sketch of le Nôtre by Desgodetz, a learned and able architect of the time. Fifty years later Voltaire[1] called Versailles " un chef-d'œuvre de mauvais goût et de magnificence " and its chapel " ce colifichet fastueux

> qui du peuple éblouit les yeux
> et dont le connoisseur se raille."

At the same time, owing to the glory of its gardens by le Nôtre, and the inimitable craftsmanship throughout, Versailles is in its way unique, and the perfect embodiment for good or bad of the art of the reign of Louis XIV.

Not content with all that was being done at Versailles,

[1] " Le Temple du Goust," 1733. " chez Hierosme Print-all."

on which over 25 million francs had been spent by
1680, the King did not hesitate to embark on a fresh
enterprise at Marly, eight kilometres from Versailles.
Here he found a valley, a " repaire (haunt) des serpents
et charognes (corpses), des crapauds (toads) et des gren-
ouilles (frogs)."[1]   The soil was so bad that according to
the author of *The Theory and Practice of Gardening*,
published at Paris in 1709, fruit grown at Marly was
bitter to the taste, but confident that he could do anything, the King instructed Mansart to design one
of the most idiotic country-houses ever conceived by
man.   The valley was converted into a building site
with banks sloping down to a level garden with a waterpiece down the centre.   At the upper end was placed
the King's house and along two sides were ranged
twelve separate houses, six on each side, intended for
the lodgment of courtiers and symbolizing the planets
attending on le Roi Soleil.   The total cost of Marly
between 1679 and 1695 as given in the *Comptes des
Bâtiments du Roi* was 11,611,918 fr. 18s. 5d.   Fontainebleau, St. Germain and " diverses maisons royales "
all had to be maintained, and the total cost of Versailles, the Grand Trianon and Clagny, 1664-1715, was

[1] Saint-Simon.

64,580,565 fr. 14s. 6d., estimated as equivalent to some £13,000,000 sterling. I visited Marly in 1921 and excepting " l'abreuvoir," the drinking-place at the lower end, there is not a trace of building left, the terraces and waterpiece are now all covered with grass, and what were once avenues, pleached groves and alleys, are now woods on the hillside.

Mansart was employed at Chantilly, and between 1680-88 seems to have monopolised the whole official architecture of France. Bruand was still engaged on the Invalides, but Mansart, once his pupil and assistant, came in over his head in 1680, and was commissioned to design the second church, the Church of the Dome, under which lies the tomb of Napoleon. The interior is admirable, and from certain points of view the dome of the Invalides is very effective, but it cannot compare with Wren's design of St. Paul's as executed. The dome of the Invalides stands up like an isolated monument, too high and top-heavy for the substructure. Wren in his design of St. Paul's built up an admirable architectural composition leading up to the drum and dome as its culminating point. Mansart seems to have thought only of the dome, and more or less left the rest of the building to take care of itself. Mansart designed the Place Vendôme in 1690-91, St. Cyr, Dampierre and other houses, and his last work was the chapel at Versailles. He died suddenly in 1708, having just lasted out his great reputation and only escaping by his death from a prosecution for embezzlement.

So far as his career was concerned, Mansart was probably the most successful architect that has ever lived. When he died he was Chevalier de l'Ordre de St. Michel, Comte de Sagonne, surintendant et ordonna-teur de ses (the King's) bâtiments et ses jardins aussi que des arts et manufactures royales," a post probably worth not less than some £12,000 [1] a year, with infinite possibilities of commissions and patronage, and he was also director of the Academies of painting, sculpture and architecture, practically in control of all the arts of France. With all his multifarious appointments, and with the constant necessity of keeping himself well to the fore and preserving his position with the King, it is quite certain that Mansart could not possibly have designed all the work attributed to him ; and that was the opinion of his contemporaries, but he had working for him some of the ablest young architects of his time, such as

[1] His official salaries as given in the *Comptes des Bâtiments du Roi* in 1699 mounted to 60,866 livres.

LES INVALIDES. CHURCH OF THE DOME

PLACE VENDÔME

Desgodetz, Daviler, l'Assurance and de Cotte, and it appears that his habit was to make rough sketches and leave the rest to his draughtsmen. That he was either very ignorant of construction or very careless is shown by the failures of his bridges. A bridge designed by him collapsed at Blois, so did the bridge at Moulins. Saint-Simon relates that when Louis XIV inquired about the bridge at Moulins, the governor of the province replied that he understood that it had last been heard of at Nantes. It was in consequence of these failures that the department of "Ponts et Chaussées" was established. The State had suffered dearly from the extravagance and carelessness of Mansart, who was too busy with his own interests to attend to his work. Saint-Simon says that most of his work was done by an architect " sous clef," and it seems probable that he was only saved from disaster by his very competent staff, and the admirable technique of the craftsmen at his command. For nearly all the work attributed to him is of consummate technical excellence, but Jules Hardouin Mansart was not an artist when all is said. " Ce maçon," as Saint-Simon contemptuously calls him, " ce gros homme bien fait, d'un visage agréable, et de la lie du peuple," must have been a very able man to win and maintain his position in the court of Louis XIV for something like forty years, but like John Nash, " the Stucco King" of a later date, he was impudent, audacious, and unscrupulous, perhaps the most conspicuous example of the architect " entrepreneur "; of the man whose heart is set not on architecture, but on his own personal interests, a great position and a lucrative practice.

After twenty years of unrestrained extravagance in building by Louis XIV, aided and abetted by J. H. Mansart, the possibilities of building were pretty well exhausted by the end of the seventeenth century. M. Guiffrey, the editor of the *Comptes des Bâtiments du Roi*, says that from 1690 onwards the State was hardly able to find the money to maintain the royal palaces and establishments such as the Gobelins and the French Academy at Rome, which depended on State subsidies for their very existence. The brilliant promise of the early years of the reign was not realized. The King's vanity and ambition were landing him in all sorts of difficulties, and there was no money available, for by 1690 the King and his courtiers had built themselves to the verge of bankruptcy. Moreover, the political and social conditions of France steadily grew worse and worse. The solemn hypocrisy of the latter days of Louis XIV was followed by the licence of the Regent, the disastrous financial juggling of Law and the gross egotism of Louis XV. Throughout the eighteenth century the menace of imminent catastrophe was becoming ever more insistent, and when it came the splendid tradition of French architecture, a tradition built up by many generations, was lost for ever. At the same time, Colbert's work was built upon a solid foundation, and the lines that he laid down in his reorganization of the arts of France remained more or less unaltered till the latter part of the eighteenth century. The result was a very high level of technical competence, but the independence and adventure of an earlier age were lost for ever.

A LIST OF TYPICAL BUILDINGS
1661–1708

Versailles.
The Louvre (east front).
Collége des Quatre Nations (Institut de France), 1660-72.
La Rochelle. La Porte Royale.
Porte St. Martin, 1674, Paris.
Porte St. Denis, 1673, Paris.
Porte St. Antoine, 1672, Paris.
Hotel des Invalides, 1675, Paris.

MANSART'S CAREER

La Salpêtrière, 1678, Paris.
Place Vendôme, 1691, Paris.
Hotel de Beauvais, Paris.
Hotel de Hollande or Bizeuil, Paris.
Sceaux, 1673 (destroyed).
Meudon (destroyed).
Marly, 1679 (destroyed).
Clagny, 1676 (destroyed).
Saint Cloud Gardens—house destroyed 1870.
Choisy-le-Roi (destroyed).
Maintenon, the Aqueduct, 1685.
Chantilly, the gardens, from 1663.
Les Invalides, Mansart's church, 1683.
Saint Cyr, 1685.
Hotel de Ville, Arles, 1684.
Tours, Tribunal de Commerce and Préfecture.
Valognes, Hôtel de Beaumont.
Lyon, Hôtel de Ville.
Hôtel de Ville, Dijon, 1682 and 1708.
Dampierre, 1680.
Notre Dame de la Gloriette, Caen, 1684-89.
Montpellier, Château d'Eau, 1689.
    Porte du Peyrou, 1692.
Abbeville, Hôtel de Ville, 1685.
    The Carpet Factory.
Lille, Porte de Paris, 1682, and Porte de Tournai.
Hôtel de Soubise, 1706 (Archives Nationales).
Hôtel de Nevers (Bibliothèque Nationale).

All dates approximate only.

ILLUSTRATIONS

Chap. V. Illustrations.

Versailles (the orangery).
    do.   (the chapel).
Les Invalides, Church of the Dome.
Place Vendôme.
Maintenon, the Aqueduct.
The Petit Trianon.

CHAPTER VI

Mansart's Successors. L'Assurance, le Roux, de Cotte. Aubert. Daviler. Desgodetz. Delamaire. The Hôtel de Soubise. Boffrand's designs for Prince Bishops and Electors. Aubert and Chantilly. Oppenord. The Cuviliés. Servandoni. Héré. His work at Nancy.

Jules Hardouin Mansart died in 1708, having outlived his own reputation and his period, for the immense building activity of the earlier years of the reign of Louis XIV came to an end about the year 1690-91. Thirty years' extravagance had exhausted the savings of Mazarin, and after 1690 the King had other things to think of. Mme de Maintenon had established her disastrous ascendancy over the King. Then came the troubles of the Spanish Succession and Marlborough's victorious campaigns. The treasury was empty and a few years later most of those who had not wasted their substance in building to please the King, were ruined by Law's fantastic finance in 1716. The decorators were active and very accomplished, but compared with the seventeenth century not much building was done, and the leading French architects had to look to prince-bishops and electors, who called them in to design immense palaces in the French manner, but seldom paid them for their labours.

The Mansart dynasty was carried on by his staff, l'Assurance, le Roux, de Cotte and Aubert. Neither Daviler nor Desgodetz, both of whom had been working for Mansart, left their mark on the architecture of the time ; yet both were accomplished architects and draughtsmen. Finding that there was no room in Paris for anyone but Mansart, Daviler retired to Montpellier, where he carried out the Porte du Peyrou, and the attractive Château d'Eau, and wrote an excellent treatise on architecture. He died young in 1700. Desgodetz, to whom I attribute the Orangery at Versailles, was a beautiful draughtsman who probably knew more about the details of Roman architecture than Mansart, de Cotte and the whole Academy of Architecture put together. His work, " Les Edifices Antiques de Rome," was remarkable not only for the immense labour of its preparation, but also for its consummate draughtsmanship, and I doubt if there has ever been made a finer set of measured drawings of architecture. " Pierre Cailleteau dit l'Assurance " built many hôtels in Paris after 1700, and was probably the most capable of Mansart's numerous staff. He, Aubert and le Roux were typical of the successful French architects of the first half of the eighteenth century. Good men of affairs, skilful planners and competent designers, the obedient servants of the corrupt but cheerful society of the time, they seem to have been architects without very high ideals or any particular convictions, and it took two generations to recover from the deadly influence of Jules Hardouin Mansart.

The best of them was undoubtedly Robert de Cotte, born in 1656. About the year 1685 he married Mansart's sister-in-law, Catharine Bodin. Two years later through Mansart's influence he was made an Academician and in 1699 was appointed an " architecte du Roi " and director of the Academy of Architecture. On Mansart's death in 1708 he succeeded him as " premier architecte du Roi," finished the chapel at Versailles, and designed the high altar of Notre Dame in Paris, to take the place of a design made by Mansart fifteen years before which was so bad that it was stopped at once. Mansart had done well for his relations, for by 1708 de Cotte was in receipt of an annual salary of nearly 30,000 francs a year with 4000 francs a year for his

HÔTEL DE SOUBISE (EXTERIOR)

HÔTEL DE SOUBISE (INTERIOR)

son, an incompetent youth of twenty. After Mansart's death, he was recognized as the leading architect of his time and was in great request both in France and in foreign countries. In 1712 he prepared a scheme for rebuilding the palace of Buen Retiro near Madrid, to suggestions made by that able lady, the Princesse des Ursins. In the year following he was called in by Joseph Clement, Elector of Cologne, to design various houses. The Elector was extremely anxious to be in the fashion, but hoped to be so at other people's expense. De Cotte prepared designs for a villa on the Rhine, and for rebuilding the castle of Poppelsdorf, and for a palace at Bonn. The work at Bonn was put in hand and is an interesting and characteristic building with an inner circular court, but the Elector never paid up, and de Cotte was advised by his representatives in Germany not to supply any more details till he did. De Cotte prepared designs for the château of Frescati, near Metz, for the duc de Coislin, Bishop of Metz, a building destroyed in 1800 and said to have cost 1,200,000 livres. He was employed by the Bishop of Verdun in 1725 to design him a vast palace, and in 1728 by Cardinal Armand Gaston Maximilian de Rohan, Bishop of Strasbourg, to make some extensive additions to his château of Saverne, now best known for the episode of " the Captain of Zaberne." Saverne is about halfway between Nancy and Strasbourg. The château was turned into barracks, and little is left but remains of two façades and gardens once of great magnificence. These prince bishops and electors regarded their bishoprics solely as a source of income for their personal expenditure, and very seldom made a serious attempt to discharge their liabilities or pay their architects. Of de Cotte's work in Paris the most famous was the decoration of the Hôtel de Toulouse. He died in 1735, not perhaps a great architect, but shrewd and adroit, and Blondel says that he was a man of honour and humanity.

The architect who most resembled de Cotte was Germain Boffrand, born at Nantes in 1667, and trained in Mansart's office. He designed several hôtels in Paris, including the Hôtel Amelot in the rue Saint Dominique which is remarkable for its oval court and very interesting plan, and the decorations of the Hôtel de Soubise (now Archives Nationales) which had been built in 1706 from the designs of Delamaire. The decorations of the Hôtel de Soubise are very attractive in their way, but as was said by critics at the time it is not the way of architecture. The cornice has ceased to exist and the walls run out into the ceiling behind a camouflage of quirks and twirligigs without any logical justification. The odd thing is that when these decorations were executed, Boffrand was becoming an old man, and they are quite unlike his rather heavy architecture. He must have been caught in the shortlived fashion for the Baroque set by Oppenord, Meissonnier and Cuviliés, and not yet exploded by Nicholas Cochin in the *Mercure de Paris*, 1750-52, for later on Boffrand himself condemned this fashion for torturing buildings into abnormal shapes in which " la bizarrerie est admirée sous le nom de génie." The Hôtel de Soubise is still one of the best examples of its kind, quite admirable in execution, and in good hands this manner has a fascination of its own. The most austere formalist will find it hard to resist the attractions of buildings such as the Amalienburg in the grounds of the Nymphenburg Palace at Munich, that dainty little hunting-lodge, built by an elector to amuse his wife, with its decorations in blue, canary, and silver, but François Cuviliés had a genius for this work, and in clumsy hands it is very soon intolerable. Moreover it offended the deep-seated French instinct for pure form, and it went out of fashion after the middle of the eighteenth century. There is little

trace of it in the work of the Gabriels, father and son.
It was altogether too trivial for their robust and mascu-
line intelligence. Meanwhile Boffrand was extensively
employed on designing enormous houses between
1720-40, and he published a book of his designs for
various German princes, which includes a vast hunting-
lodge with a central circular hall 60 feet in diameter with
a look-out above it 120 feet high, and palaces at Nancy,
Malgrange, Lunéville and Würzburg, all on a gigantic
scale and never completed. He entered for the famous
competition of 1748 for the Place Louis XV (now Place
de la Concorde), but was unsuccessful. Boffrand died in
1754, aged 88, having lost most of his money in specu-
lation, and been unable to retrieve his fortunes by the
miniatures and snuffboxes with which princes and
bishops were in the habit of rewarding his services. He
appears to have been an excellent sort of man, a very
human and irresponsible person of a rare and attractive
type. Like Vanbrugh, but with less ability, Boffrand
wrote plays, and like Vanbrugh he suffered from a
megalomania which seems to have grown on him with
advancing years. Boffrand, with less ability and less
imagination than Vanbrugh, had more knowledge of
technique, but it appears both from his writings and his

CHANTILLY. THE STABLES

ST. SULPICE

works that he never went to the heart of the matter, never realized that architecture is not play-acting, but a serious art limited by practical conditions.

Servandoni (1695-1766), an Italian born at Florence, also seems to have arrived at architecture by way of the theatre, for he made his reputation by his skill in designing theatrical scenery, and staging " spectacles," and he was the greatest showman of the eighteenth century. He is said to have designed the scenery for more than sixty operas with scenes ranging from the palace of Nineveh to the mosque of Scanderbeg. In 1731 he was admitted a member of the Academy of Painting, and presented as his diploma work a picture of ruins, an anticipation of the subjects which Hubert Robert was to find so profitable later on. In 1732 he won the competition for the completion of St. Sulpice in Paris, and the west front was carried out from his designs. After this he seems to have given up architecture and devoted himself to stage design. In 1738 a series of prodigious " spectacles " was given in the Salle des Machines in the Tuileries. The Pope made him a count of the Order of St. John Lateran and a member of the military Order of Christ. In 1749 he was invited to London to direct the illuminations to celebrate the peace of Aix-la-Chapelle, and he seems to have been invited to most of the courts of Europe, including Vienna, and to have nearly ruined the duke of Würtemburg. He had immense opportunities, but "ce génie rare et excellent," as Blondel calls him, was hopelessly generous and improvident, and died a poor man in 1766.

Delamaire's reputation rests chiefly on his first design for the Hôtel de Soubise (Archives Nationales) ; Jean Aubert's on the amazing stables that he designed for the duc de Bourbon at Chantilly. The duc had made an immense fortune in the Mississippi Company under Law's " system " just before the collapse of that financier in 1720, and he proceeded to spend it on these stables, 579 feet long by 56 feet wide by 42 feet 6 inches high with huge pavilions in the centre and at the ends. The stables provided stalls for 240 horses. The stalls, it is true, were only 4 feet 6 inches wide, but the plump French horses were no doubt glad of support, and economy here left Aubert free to give the stables of Chantilly the most magnificent façade of any building of their kind that has ever been built. Aubert's work on the stables at Chantilly is more brilliant than anything by Mansart at Versailles, and apart from their plan, the stables at Chantilly are perhaps the finest example now existing of French architecture in the grand manner.

Jean Courtonne (1671-1739) and Jean Silvan Cartaud (1675-1758) were famous architects in their day. Blondel thought highly of them, but they are now just names. Apart from the two Gabriels among the architects, and Oppenord, Cuviliés and Meissonnier among the decorators, the most distinguished French architect in the eighteenth century was not a Parisian but, like Wood of Bath, a provincial architect. Emmanuel Héré de Corny was born at Lunéville in 1705, the son of an official in the service of the Duke of Lorraine. In 1745, Stanislas Leczinsky, titular King of Poland, having no kingdom and little to do, began a grand scheme of town-planning at Nancy. There were then two separate towns, the old town to the north dating from the twelfth century, and the new town begun in the sixteenth century, near the unfinished palace that Boffrand had designed for the Duke of Lorraine. Between the towns was an unoccupied open space and Héré's problem was to link up the two towns. He began at the south end with the fine square of the Place Royale, with buildings on three sides. The side opposite the Hôtel de Ville was left free and opened on to the Place de la Carrière, 810 feet long by 180 feet wide. At the end of the Carrière he formed the " Hémicycle," a " place " 300 feet long with hemicycles at each end. From this one passes to the Hôtel de l'Intendance and gardens beyond once laid out in the manner of le Nôtre, but since destroyed by the landscape gardener. Altogether a masterly design admirable in detail and Héré's work at Nancy is one of the best things of its kind in France, carried out at less than half the cost of Marly. The whole scheme is delightfully simple and logical, and yet so varied in detail that it is full of unexpected charm. Keenly alive to balance and symmetry, Héré played with perfect mastery on motives that in less competent hands would have seemed exuberant and out of place. His work at Nancy remains a masterpiece, less extensive but more sumptuous than what the elder Wood did at Bath for Ralph Allen. Héré holds a place of honour among the great French architects of the eighteenth century, but of himself little is known except that he was the father of sixteen children, that he finally went out of his mind and died at Lunéville in 1763 at the age of 57.

Héré's work at Nancy is of peculiar interest in

NANCY. THE HEMICYCLE

MONTPELLIER. THE CHÂTEAU D'EAU

another way as evidence of artistic intelligence outside Paris. De Brosses in his letters from Italy (1740) pointed out how poor Paris was in the "manière de disposer les points de vue," vistas and perspectives, and that except the Place Vendôme and the Place Royale, there was nothing to compare with what he saw at Rome, for the Place Louis XV (Place de la Concorde) did not exist when he wrote. But in the provinces some admirable examples of civic improvement and town-planning date from the eighteenth century. The Promenade de Peyrou at Montpellier is an early example. At Orléans, Saumur, and Tours, vistas in connection with roads and bridges were deliberately planned. There are fine " places " and promenades at Bordeaux, Périgueux and Amiens, and that remarkable " Promenade des Terreaux " in the little town of Avallon (Yonne) laid out and planted in 1720. At Aix-en-Provence there is a characteristic example of an eighteenth-century promenade, which de Brosses describes. " Les maisons sont hautes, belles, et à l'italienne. Quatre rangs d'arbres y forment deux contre-allées où l'on se promène, et une longue allée au milieu ornée de quatre grandes fontaines." In the preface to his " Monumens érigés en France à la Gloire de Louis

XV " (1765) Patte refers with pride to the public works carried out in the provinces in the reign of Louis XV, such as the quays on the banks of the Rhône and Saône and the Hospital with a façade nearly 900 feet long at Lyon. Nantes, he says, had been transformed almost into a new town. Nancy, Lunéville and Commercy, " enfin toute la Lorraine," had been altered out of knowledge, and changes scarcely less important had been carried out at Besançon, Metz, La Rochelle, Rennes, Alençon, Tours, Caen, Rouen, Dijon, Nîmes, Montpellier, Aix, Lille, Valenciennes, Reims, Versailles and elsewhere. Triumphal arches,—not always very happy,—were built wherever possible, and the department of Ponts et Chaussées, established by Trudaine in 1743, was busily employed in improving the roads and bridges of France. Mansart's failures had shown the urgent necessity of more scientific bridge building, and Patte says that at the beginning of the eighteenth century, there were only four " grandes routes bien pavées " in France. The serious attempt at public improvement and town-planning was perhaps the most important advance made by French architecture in the eighteenth century.

ILLUSTRATIONS

Chap. VI.   Illustrations.

Chantilly, the Stables.
Hôtel de Soubise, exterior.
   (Archives Nationales), interior.
Nancy, the Hemicycle.
St. Sulpice.
Montpellier, the Château d'Eau.

CHAPTER VII

The Gabriels, Jacques Jules. The Bridge and the Evêché at Blois.
Rennes, the Hôtel de Ville. Bordeaux. Place de la Bourse.
La Rochelle, the Cathedral. Ange Jacques Gabriel. The com-
petition for the Place de la Concorde. The Ecole Militaire. The
Petit Trianon. The last of the old Régime. Soufflot and the
Panthéon. Contant d'Ivry. Patte. Mique. Louis. The end
of a great period. Examples.

With the exception of Héré, who corresponds to our
Wood of Bath, de Cotte and Aubert the magnificent, the work of the Epigoni, the architects who carried
on after the great outburst of building for Louis XIV
had died away, is not very interesting. It was perfectly
accomplished but not always convincing, and it is
marked by a lack of enterprise that on occasion makes
it even tedious, better than the " pompier " manner of
the nineteenth century, but only because it was in
better taste, and altogether superior in technique. Two
men stand out conspicuously among the French architects of the eighteenth century, the two Gabriels,
father and son. Jacques Jules Gabriel, the father, was

BORDEAUX. HÔTEL DE LA BOURSE

LA ROCHELLE. THE CATHEDRAL

born in 1667, the son of a mason contractor whose wife was a cousin of J. H. Mansart. In 1687 Gabriel's father bought him the post of " Contrôleur général alternatif des Bastimens " from Mansart for 90,000 francs, a characteristic instance of Mansart's cupidity, and of the opportunities of jobbery that existed in spite of Colbert's efforts, for Gabriel was only twenty at the time. His first known work was Choisi, a great house on the banks of the Seine, for Mlle de Montpensier, with gardens laid out by le Nôtre. He designed some important but not very interesting houses in Paris, and his best work was done in the provinces. So far, building enterprise had been limited to royal palaces and great houses within a few miles of Paris. The Invalides was the one effort of Louis XIV in public buildings. The Regency had neither the money nor the inclination to do anything, and it was not till the reign of Louis XV, with all his faults, that any serious attempt was made to carry out necessary public works such as bridges, and to improve disorderly cities by consecutive and considered schemes of architecture. Jacques Jules Gabriel was a pioneer in this work. In 1716 he designed the great bridge at Blois and the fine Evêché, bridges at Poissy, Charenton, Pontoise, Saint Maur and elsewhere, and in 1720, after a great fire at Rennes in Brittany, he was called in to design the Hôtel de Ville, one of the most attractive eighteenth-century municipal buildings in France. This was followed in 1728 by his memorable work at Bordeaux, the Place Royale (now Place de la Bourse) on the quay overlooking the river—a splendid example of civic architecture. His last work was the fine cathedral church of La Rochelle. Gabriel died at Fontainebleau in 1742, full of honours : " Sieur de Berney, premier architecte du Roi, Inspecteur Général des Bâtiments du Roi," the ablest architect that had appeared in France since the days of François Mansart. Only one architect in the eighteenth century surpassed him and that was his son, Ange Jacques Gabriel, born in 1698.

At the age of thirty Ange Jacques Gabriel married the daughter of the first secretary of the duc d'Antin, Directeur Général des Bâtiments, and was admitted to the second class of the Academy. In 1742 he succeeded his father as " premier architecte du Roi ", and his career was one of uninterrupted success. He was employed at Versailles, Marly, Choisi, and Compiègne, and he had to attend to the royal princesses, and the far more exacting demands of Madame de Pompadour and Madame du Barry. His employment at Versailles must have been exasperating in the last degree with its constant changes, cancelled orders and lack of money. About the middle of the eighteenth century he re-modelled much of the interior of the palace, and pre-pared a scheme known as the "Grand projet," for the removal of the Cour de Marbre, the last vestige of the old hunting-lodge of Louis XIII and the erection of a new façade on the entrance front. This scheme was dropped, but the Salle de l'Opéra was completed in 1766, after hanging fire for some twenty years. It is not the happiest of Gabriel's works, but it was starved by the chronic lack of money, indeed in 1773 the work at Versailles was so slow that Mme du Barry wanted Gabriel to throw the contractor into prison. His real opportunity came in 1748. In that year a grand com-petition was held for a monument to Louis XV. The idea was to celebrate the virtues of "un bon prince, un vrai héros de l'humanité," so Patte calls him the "hero" of Mme de Pompadour, the Parc aux Cerfs and Mme du Barry. Monuments were begun but not always completed at Bordeaux, Valenciennes, Rennes, Nancy, Reims and Rouen, as well as at Paris. Apparently no specific programme was laid down and

anybody could suggest what they liked. All the architects of the Academy were invited to compete and over
fifty designs were submitted. The first difficulty was
to find a site, and to solve the difficulty the King presented to the city a waste piece of ground lying between
the Tuileries gardens and the Champs Elysées. A
fresh competition was held, and all the architects of the
Academy except eight competed. De Cotte declined,
saying he was too old. None of the designs was considered to be quite satisfactory. Marigny, the director-
general, produced a design of his own, which he
assured Louis XV combined every merit, but the King
was no fool and in the result he appointed Gabriel to
make a " réunion " of all the best points in the plans
submitted, and to carry out the work, a grossly unfair
proceeding, but one which resulted in the finest public
" place " in France, and one of the finest in the world,
the Place de la Concorde. Gabriel's design for the
Champs Elysées was never carried out, with the result that
a great opportunity was lost, and the existing Place de la
Concorde has been so much altered that it does far less
than justice to Gabriel's layout ; but his splendid buildings on the north side still remain to show something
of what might have been but for the nineteenth century.

ÉCOLE MILITAIRE

THE ÉCOLE MILITAIRE

The École Militaire, with the Petit Trianon at Versailles, the greatest of Gabriel's works, was begun in 1751, but it was carried on under great difficulties and not finished till 1773. Incomplete as it is, the École Militaire is the noblest example of Neo-classic architecture in Paris, the last word of a magnificent tradition that it had taken over two hundred years to form and which never ought to have been abandoned. The Petit Trianon, begun in 1763 for Madame du Barry, was one of the latest of Gabriel's works, and sums up all the great qualities of his design, his instinct for proportion, his power of selection, his restraint and the sureness of his taste.

Gabriel retired from practice in 1775 and died in 1782. Like Sir William Chambers in England, he was " ultimus Romanorum," the last of the traditionalists. He was a great architect, and a strong fearless man who went his own way, and was resolute enough to resist the intrigues of Marigny, backed by his allpowerful sister, Madame de Pompadour. Gabriel was the last undeviating adherent of the national tradition of his country in architecture, but the control was slipping out of the hands of architects into those of amateurs such as the Comte de Caylus, and after the Revolution, of pedants such as Quatremère de Quincy.

THE END OF A GREAT TRADITION

Nicholas Cochin in his memoir of the Comte de Caylus says, " Les gens de condition (a characteristic eighteenth-century phrase) font sans doute honneur aux corps auxquels ils s'attachent, mais le malheur est qu'ils le savent trop bien, et qu'il est rare que leur protection ne dégénère pas en quelque peu de tyrannie." The Comte de Caylus was a vain, arbitrary and vindictive amateur, and the French Academies of Painting and Sculpture paid dearly for placing their necks under his heel. The Academy of Architecture had the good sense to keep him at arm's length, but the amateur was steadily encroaching on the province of the expert. Till Voltaire and Diderot, literary men had left the arts alone. It is true there were treatises on architecture in abundance ; they were written by architects and rather dull, but the Romantic movement was advancing fast. It broke through the thin barrier of technical knowledge and treated the arts as free for all, often with most amusing results, for Diderot's pungent criticisms of the Salons (1761-71) are still the best things of their kind ever written. It was a bad thing for the arts when they became what they have remained—material for copy for the literary man. Ever since those days the literary man, " the critic," has been telling artists what they ought to do and how they ought to do it. If the Comte de Caylus was bad, Quatremère de Quincy was worse, a ferocious pedant who insisted on the literal revival of the antique as then understood. When in 1791 the Constituent Assembly decided to transform Ste. Geneviève into the Panthéon, Quatremère de Quincy drew up the programme which Soufflot was to follow. The building was to be an allegorical expression of " the duties of man in society," and no artist was to be allowed to take part in the decoration who had not steeped himself in " le goût antique " as taught by Winckelmann and practised by Canova in Italy. The whole affair of the Panthéon was typical of the self-deception of the people of Paris at the end of the eighteenth century, full of misguided enthusiasm, throwing overboard all standards hitherto accepted, and accepting blindly unsound and unhistorical assumptions. Soufflot, who was a generous and enthusiastic man, might, had he been left to himself, have carried on the work of Gabriel, so too might Contant d'Ivry who designed the original church of the Madeleine in Paris, and the great cathedral at Arras, destroyed by the Germans in the late war. Contant d'Ivry, who died in 1777, a famous man in his time, is now almost forgotten, and indeed we have reached the end of a very great period of architecture. Its last official interpreter had been Jacques François Blondel (1705-74), not a great architect but a teacher and author of amazing industry, and a sound and very competent critic with a real appreciation of the finer qualities of architecture. The famous theatre at Bordeaux, built from the design of Victor Louis, 1773-80, was almost the last example of the traditional manner in France.

Pierre Patte (1722-1812) carried on Blondel's work, but the fashion had moved away from the architects to the archaeologists, and the Revolution was at hand. Richard Mique who had followed Héré at Nancy, and succeeded Gabriel as " premier architecte " of Louis XVI, was condemned as a royalist with his son on July 1794 and executed on the following day. The Academies went down with the throne, and the Revolution opened the doors to all sorts of fantastic theories in the arts as well as in literature and politics. A generation had arisen that repudiated the great tradition of French Neo-classic and believed itself to have rediscovered the secret of architecture in a slavish revival of the antique. In the introduction to a book by J. M. Peyre published in 1795, the editor asked in what age had

THE MADELEINE

THE PANTHÉON

architecture reached a higher degree of perfection, and asserted that such buildings as the Hôtel de la Monnaie,[1] the Odéon [2] and the Panthéon,[3] and the taste of the young artists of the time, were as far removed from the architecture of the beginning of the eighteenth century as that architecture was from Gothic. The immediate result was an absurdly pedantic revival of classical forms. The break with tradition meant the loss of any definite clue and standard of values, and if it was open to architects to design a hospital like a temple of Aesculapius, it was equally open to them to design a house like a medieval castle, and this they very soon proceeded to do, for the Gothic revival followed hard on the heels of Napoleonic classic, with the futile idea of bolstering up the monarchy by a medieval revival. After Chalgrin, Brongniart, Gondouin, Vignon, Percier and Fontaine, Viollet-le-Duc was inevitable with Pierrefonds and Carcassonne.

The results of this summary survey are these : The Renaissance in France in the sixteenth century is not to be regarded as an isolated movement but as the first step in a continuing development which reached its culminating point in the third quarter of the eighteenth

---

[1] Antoine, 1771.   [2] Wailly & Peyre, 1782.   [3] Soufflot.

century, when it went down before the rising tide of the Romantic movement. The three hundred years, from the date of the first Italian expedition to that of the French Revolution, include three well-marked periods, the first from the Italian expedition of 1494 to the accession of Henri IV nearly a hundred years later, the second from the beginning of the seventeenth century to about 1661, when Louis XIV began his personal rule and Colbert brought in the new régime, and the third from the advent of Colbert till the break-up of tradition in the last quarter of the eighteenth century. Each of these three periods has its subdivisions. In the earlier years of the sixteenth century, French architecture was represented by the efforts of the master-builders in the new manner with the help of the Italian ornamentalists, and the rest of the century saw the coming of the architects, who introduced formal method into what so far had been little more than a series of experiments. At the end of the sixteenth century, owing to what was almost civil war, there came a détente, but with Henri IV architecture made a fresh start, and what had so far been a fashion of the Court became a vernacular style understood and practised throughout France as a matter of course. In the reign of Louis XIII, the Italian motive reasserted itself to a considerable extent, but it was interpreted by French architects in their own individual and characteristic manner. The third period begins with the personal rule of Louis XIV, and the advent of Colbert in 1661. Architecture henceforward became official, more or less a State affair rigidly controlled. One result was to standardize French architecture, and replace the individual artist by the official architect, a loss in adventure, but the technique of architecture and the allied crafts steadily advanced, and the culminating point of Neo-classical architecture in France was reached soon after the middle of the eighteenth century, and was lost when the younger Gabriel retired from practice in 1775. After that came the deluge, pedantic archaeology instead of architecture, followed by wild and ill-conceived attempts to revive medieval methods, ending finally in the bankruptcy of architecture in the nineteenth century, and the total repudiation of the past in the twentieth. France is still very rich in examples of architecture extending over eight or nine hundred years, but it is sad to think of what she has lost. MM. de Foville and le Sourd in their handbook *Les Châteaux de France* refer to some 1670 houses as still existing, but " l'obituaire des chefs-

CONCLUSIONS

d'œuvre de l'architecture est immense ". The Château de Madrid, la Muette, the Tuileries, the chapel of the Valois, and some of the most famous seventeenth-century Hôtels in Paris have all gone, so too have great houses in the country such as Gaillon, St. Maur, Charleval and Verneuil of the sixteenth century, Monceaux, Richelieu, Berni, Liencour, Meudon, Marly, Sceaux, Choisi, Clagny, St. Cloud of the seventeenth century, and these are only a few names taken at random, but they should not be utterly forgotten. It is well nowadays to turn back from time to time to the study of the masterpieces of the past. Only in this way is it possible to form well founded standards of values, and to hand on the torch to those who will follow us.

A LIST OF TYPICAL BUILDINGS
1708–1794

Blois, the bridge, 1716.
   The Evêché.
The Stables, Chantilly, 1719-35.
Rennes, Hôtel de Ville, 1734.
Hôtel de Soubise (Archives Nationales), Interior, 1725.
Avallon, Promenade des Terreaux, 1720.
Juvisy (Seine-et-Oise), Pont des Belles Fontaines, 1728.
Bordeaux, Place de la Bourse, 1728.
St. Sulpice, Paris, façade, 1733.

CONCLUSIONS

La Rochelle, the Cathedral, 1741.

Rouen, Porte Guillaume, 1749.

Arras, the Cathedral, 1753-1833.

Place Louis XV (Place de la Concorde), 1748-72.

École Militaire, Paris, 1751-73.

Compiègne, château, begun, 1755.

Salle de l'Opéra, Versailles, 1748-66.

Petit Trianon, Versailles, 1763.

Nancy, Place Royale
   La Carrière
   The Hemicycle
   Hôtel de Ville   } 1735-1761.
   The Porte Stanislas
   Porte Desilles, the Arc de Triomphe

Toulouse, Le Capitole.

Bordeaux, Porte Dijeaux, 1748.

Rouen, Porte Guillaume, 1749.

Dijon, Porte Guillaume, 1783.

Porte Ste. Croix, Chalons-sur-Marne.

Nantes, Préfecture.

Moulins, Lycée Banville.

Menars, 1765.

Pont de Tours, 1765-76.

The Madeleine, Paris, 1764-1842.

The Panthéon, Paris, 1764, 1780.

Hôtel de la Monnaie, Paris, 1771.

The Odéon, Paris, 1782.

Bordeaux, the Theatre, 1773-1780.

All dates approximate only.

ILLUSTRATIONS

INDEX

[123]

INDEX

INDEX

INDEX

[126]

INDEX

INDEX

INDEX

www.ingramcontent.com/pod-product-compliance
Lightning Source LLC
Chambersburg PA
CBHW021143090426
42740CB00008B/920